# THE MEANING OF LIFE

3092-EVER

# THE
# MEANING OF
# LIFE

*A Practical Guide
to Staying Alive*

## Louis Everstine

3092-EVER

Library of Congress Number:        00-192656
ISBN #:            Hardcover        0-7388-4610-4
                   Softcover        0-7388-4611-2

This book was printed in the United States of America.

Cover photograph from the "Mirage" series of Judith M. Walker.

Portrait of the author by André Monjoin.

Index by Chris Welsh.

**To order additional copies of this book, contact:**
Xlibris Corporation
1-888-7-XLIBRIS
www.Xlibris.com
Orders@Xlibris.com

For Sunny, who found the love in me

# ACKNOWLEDGMENTS

This book was written in tribute to six persons now departed, whom I shall never forget: Daphne and Bertl and Ernst, who could have but didn't, and Phyllis and Aaron and Chris, who needn't have but did—commit suicide, that is. Not many people have met someone who was an eventual suicide, or so they tell me, but I have, and I mourn their loss as friends.

I have never attended a conference of suicidologists, nor do I plan to do so. In general, their lot is not a happy one, because they have toiled so long without success, and so many attempts at theory-making have fallen on stony ground. (One exception was Richard Seiden, a professor of mine at Berkeley, who welcomed new ideas and could even tolerate my wild speculations on the subject; many thanks.) Mostly academics, suicidologists recruit cadres of graduate students to do their "research" on suicide, the one phenomenon on which there can be no true experiment. This irony is lost on them, but they would probably learn more by contemplating their own thoughts and feelings—asking, for example, "If I committed suicide, why would it be?" Instead, they indulge themselves in the only possible source of information left to them, the "psychological autopsy," in which they sift through the leavings of people who have killed themselves, in search of clues to motives. But, alas, just as a coroner can tell us how a person died but not why, our scholars can know no more than the suicide wanted to be known.

Beyond the groves of academe, there is an army of mental health workers who have actually met a suicidal person before the fact. I have had the pleasure of speaking on the subject to a few of them, in seminars and workshops both in this country and abroad. Sunny and I have been honored guests of the distinguished therapists Pierre and Sylvie Angel, Anne Ancelin Schützenberger, and the late Catherine Mesnard in France, Mony Elkaim in Belgium, Hermann Vergouwen and Bert Van Luyn in the Netherlands, Bjorn Reigstad and Knut Sørgaard in Norway, and the staff of Centro Para El Desarrollo Y La Investigacion De La Psicoterapia Sistemica in Mexico City. Closer to home, in workshops and seminars at Kaiser Santa Teresa in San Jose and at the Mental Research Institute, I have had an opportunity to share my views on suicide with professionals who may have known what it was like to hear a threat of suicide from a client, and were forced to take responsibility not just for the person's mental health but for his or her life. They know that a threat of suicide in therapy changes therapy forever, because now the therapist is being asked to become a Lifesaver.

My views of suicide are well known to many friends and acquaintances, as I have trumpeted them for thirty years. My views of life are known to very few, and these include my good friends Cap and Jan Offut, Freda Carpenter, my cousin Eleanor Carter, and above all Barbette Mylar, who, while preparing this manuscript, read every word. Finally, at Xlibris, Jeanne Benzel was a fountain of advice and assistance.

# LISTEN

All Earth's people born to leave,
All God's children meant to grieve.

The night train waits in the station,
And the pallbearers
Bear the ones who are going
Past the ones sorrowing on.

And when the bells tell
That the train
Is moving, moving,
Faster moving,

Only the dying hear.

# PREFACE

There was a child's diversion whose name I don't recall, in which a person would link both hands together, knuckles facing upward and thumbs making a triangle, and say "Here is the church and here is the steeple. Open the door and see the people." When the hands were inverted, the fingers would wiggle, showing the people inside the church, and the children would laugh and try it themselves. I have never lost the capacity to wonder, nor my fascination with hidden secrets such as you find in Chinese boxes that open to boxes further within.

When I hear people quote Winston Churchill's famous description of Soviet Russia as "a riddle wrapped in a mystery inside an enigma," I ask myself "What is the riddle?" As a form of puzzle, the riddle has a rich history. The Greek poet, Homer, is said to have died of disappointment at not being able to solve a riddle. In legend, Oedipus solved the Riddle of the Sphinx. In Puccini's "Turandot," the hero wins the heart of a princess by solving three riddles that many former suitors lost their lives because they couldn't solve. Shakespeare was a master riddler, who embellished many of his plays with verbal conundrums such as when Macbeth is told that "none of woman born shall harm Macbeth"; he challenges Macduff, telling him "I bear a charmed life," only to learn too late that Macduff was "born" by cesarean section. A magic trick is like a riddle in that you think you see everything that is happening before you, but in fact you see nothing of what is really happening.

As a way of introducing the reader to the theme of this book, I thought of this riddle:

Death gives lessons.
Life asks Death for a lesson.
What does Death teach Life?

Answer: Everything.

I did not start this work with the intention of discovering the meaning of life, as confessed in more detail in the book that follows. Some people have studied life straightforwardly, as it presents itself to them, more or less as one would take a photograph of something and then examine it under a microscope. Others have looked for life's meaning in the mirror of death, as, for example, in "A Christmas Carol," when Ebeneezer Scrooge is forced by the ghost to look at his grave and think about what has gone before. I came to this subject from a different route. As a student of suicide, I thought about what a psychotherapist could do to prevent an act like that by a client, and then I wondered what an ordinary person could do to prevent the suicide of a relative or friend. In the process, I realized that this study had brought me near to the core of the mystery—nearer, I often thought, than I dared to go. I found, to begin with, that it is not death that reveals life's secret. Instead, it is *willful* death.

Most people think of suicide as the last refuge of a coward, but I have come to see it as more evil than that, and, paradoxically, a gift from the gods. To take the last point first, if we *could not* kill ourselves, if our brains were programmed to make the thought of it unthinkable, we could not take pride in our stoic nature, for one thing. No matter what misfortune life has dealt us, we soldier on, even though we could "end it all" in the blink of an eye. If we are honest with ourselves, when we hear of the suicide of a prominent person, we must admit to a certain feeling of superiority; at least, we have never been *that* miserable. Suicide is valuable to us, as an act, because we can do it but don't. Even so, it is far more valuable to us as a concept, because it sets our thoughts on a constructive course—as this book proves.

Suicide is evil because it hurts people who don't deserve punishment so cruel. As the philosopher said: "The useful is the good and the hurtful the base." Quite apart from any benefit it may confer on mankind, such as making us feel self-righteous or forcing us to count our blessings, willful death is the most satanic of human actions. It creates more havoc than murder, leaving more suffering in its wake. That's why, all things considered, we would rather not think about it.

Nature has a way of hiding its most intimate secrets in places guarded by unacceptable thoughts or by the human tendency to skepticism; familiar examples are electricity, the properties of the atom, and DNA. Sometimes it is necessary to keep on flying the kite in the thunderstorm, or press on when a single helix will not suffice, to reach a solution by redefining the problem. With the question of life, the requisite "paradigm shift" occurs when we alter our perception of suicide as life's *negation*, to concentrate on staying alive as life's *affirmation*. What do we affirm by greeting each new day with great expectations? What does our determination to keep on living prove? Or, by turning the coin to its other side, what does the omnipresent possibility of self-inflicted death mean to our everyday lives? The difference is as simple, for example, as driving *across*, instead of *to*, the Golden Gate Bridge.

In many ways, this is a book about death. What I think about death is of no importance; the reader's view of death is likely as valid as mine. Since we face the same prospect, the subject of death has never been far from our thoughts, throughout our lives until now. It occurs to me that a ten-year-old child is an expert on death, because he or she will have pondered every facet of the subject by that time. I can tell you one insight that came to me at the end of writing this book: *my death does not belong to me*. With this as a mantra, I urge you to read on.

Atherton
20 September 2000

# THE MEANING OF LIFE

# I. INTRODUCTION

Where Do We Come From?
What Are We?
Where Are We Going?

—title of painting
by Paul Gauguin

There are six billion people in the world, and everyone above the age of innocence has thought of suicide. Just as a person cannot think of life without death, one cannot think of either without thinking of suicide, because it lies between. If the impulse to suicide is dormant in nearly everyone, it resides there just the same. Naturally, very few people consider *committing* suicide, but since "the thought is father to the deed," no one is without risk. One day, the unthinkable may invade the mind, take root, and grow. The only totally irrevocable act may seem the only solution to an insolvable problem. The problem is no less than the one expressed in a question that everyone has asked: "What is my life for?" This need of each person to put a value on his or her life is a starting-point for the book that follows here. Six billion people can't be wrong.

When thoughts of suicide lead people to contemplate the meaning of life, they are asking themselves "What if I died today?" Because they could make that happen, they focus on the subject with a certain clarity of mind. And when they ask themselves what people will say about them when they are gone, or what will be written on their gravestones, or how they will be described in the family history, they are creating their own autobiographies. By

wishing that their legacy will be this but not that, they are defining themselves as they see themselves today, summarizing their
lives until now. This kind of self-assessment is not always harmful,
as will be shown in the pages to follow. What is ironic is that, for
many of us, only the possibility of a suicidal death can prompt
this meditation.

Along the way to insights such as those described above, we
may encounter some harsh truths about ourselves as human beings. For instance, that we are shrewd and calculating creatures,
whose dark side hides an enormous capacity for anger and feelings
of revenge. If we feel wronged, we may go to any lengths to retaliate. We are capable of acting out of spite, we hold grudges, and
some of us are prepared to use their very lives as weapons to defeat
their enemies. It is people like these, who brandish suicide as a
threat to someone else, whom the reader of this book may find
among his or her acquaintances. From people like these, as we
shall see, much can be learned.

If a person says to you "I don't want to live anymore," in one of
the many ways that people can express a thought like that, what
can you say in return? The best reply is a question, "What do you
prefer?" (Naturally, if the person is in great pain or terminally ill,
the only proper reply is "I understand"—no further questions,
case closed.) The fact is that, for most people, there just is no true
alternative to this life, and that's why the idea of dying fills most of
us with dread. Therefore, "I don't want to live anymore" is a cry for
help, and one way of responding to this cry is to interpret it as the
person's attempt to find meaning for his or her life. It has occurred
to this person that life has lost meaning, and he or she has become
seduced by the notion that, even in self-willed death, some meaning can be found. This reasoning is false if it can be shown that life
has a meaning more powerful than death, a significance beyond
the grave. What lasts forever?

# II. DEATH AS INSPIRATION

> There is but one truly serious philosophical problem,
> and that is suicide. Judging whether life is or is not worth
> living amounts to answering the fundamental question of
> philosophy. All the rest—whether or not the world has three
> dimensions, whether the mind has nine or twelve catego-
> ries—comes afterwards. These are games; one must first an-
> swer.
>
> —Albert Camus, *The Myth of Sisyphus.*

For a long time, I thought about the first sentence in *The Myth of Sisyphus*, by Albert Camus: "There is but one truly serious philo-sophical problem, and that is suicide." As a psychologist whose task it is, from time to time, to prevent someone from committing suicide, it seemed clear to me that Camus must have meant *psycho-logical* problem. Keeping your client alive is, after all, the first duty of any member of the helping professions. I wrote a book for psychotherapists, a text proposing methods that a therapist could use to deflect a person from a suicidal plan. The book was called *The Anatomy of Suicide: Silence of the Heart*; the sub-title is taken from Camus' own reflection on the suicidal act: "An act like this is prepared within the silence of the heart, as is a great work of art."

The more I read about Camus' life and work, the more I real-ized that this subject formed one of his obsessions. His most influ-ential novel, *The Stranger*, concerns a man who refuses to defend himself against a charge of murder, and allows himself to be ex-ecuted. Camus described his play about the Roman Emperor Caligula as "the story of a superior suicide." More than once in his lifetime, Camus told friends of his own thoughts about killing himself. It occurred to me that there was a connection between his own life struggles, such as the tuberculosis that plagued him from adolescence, and his preoccupation with suicide as the most "serious philosophical problem."

I believe that Camus came close to solving the "problem" that he, himself, identified. But, because of his personal fascination with the reality of suicide, he stopped short of pursuing the subject where it could lead. If you think of a door that seemed to lead the way to a valuable secret, Camus may have been reluctant to open that door. We shall never know.

I had planned to write a second book on this subject, whose original title was *Staying Alive: The Prevention of Suicide*. It was intended to be a "how-to" book, a source of practical information for people who face the dilemma of a loved-one or relative who has threatened suicide, and how to help that person stay alive. A need for this book was implied by the fact that suicide rates in America have remained stable through time, even though for forty years there has been an active academic discipline of Suicidology; in short, the root causes of suicide had not yet been discovered. This raises doubt about whether psychotherapy is effective in curing the suicidal impulse. A recent summary article on "The Assessment, Management, and Treatment of Suicidality" reached this conclusion:

> Surprisingly, relatively little is known about the actual treatment of suicidality. Little has emerged in the literature regarding effective prevention, early intervention, or treatment approaches specifically targeting those experiencing prominent suicidal ideation, exhibiting suicidal behavior, or considered at high risk to continue such behavior or eventually suicide. (Rudd. M.D., and Joiner, T. (1998) *Clinical Psychology: Science and Practice*, V5, N2, Summer, pp. 135-150.)

The journal in which this article appeared is the official organ of the discipline of clinical psychology in America. Its sad admission of the failure of the mental health establishment to find a way to prevent suicide, is not surprising at all when one considers the neglect with which the profession has treated this subject. A majority of therapists will have completed their entire training without ever taking a course on suicide; some have never read a book on the subject. Rarely does a therapist ask his or her client, "Have you ever thought of killing yourself?," or the more diplomatic "Have you thought of doing something to hurt yourself?" When the question *is* asked, and the answer is affirmative, most psychologists or counselors will refer the client to a psychiatrist to be prescribed medication. If a psychiatrist receives, from a client, an affirmative answer to the question, he or she is likely to reach for the prescription pad. A chemical solution is sought for what is believed to be the product of an imbalance in brain chemistry.

As you will see in the pages to follow, suicidal thoughts are not the product of chemistry or, for that matter, heredity or psychosis or stupidity or demonic possession. Thoughts like these have a far more insidious origin, as Camus suspected. They arise in an existential crisis of savage emotions. In their primitive fury, they reveal a fundamental truth about the human condition, as documented below.

When I began this book, I had no idea that it would lead me so far into the heart of darkness or, having gone there, that it would lead further on into light. What started as the creation of a simple, straightforward manual of how one person could prevent the death of another person, became a path toward the discovery of what life means. Setting out guidelines for the methods that would keep a life from being wasted led, by a kind of serendipity, to an understanding of what is most valuable about a life. And when one is trying to talk a suicide threatener out of committing the act, it will be necessary to show that person a reason for living, as you will see when you read the chapters below that put forth strategies of prevention.

# THE PSYCHOLOGICAL QUESTION

The most serious psychological question is: "Why do people kill themselves?" It is not whether the personality has four or five dimensions, whether schizophrenia is genetic or the product of conditioning, whether the left or right side of the brain governs emotions, or what is the best way to lead a child to calculus. The ultimate mystery is what motivates us to choose life, day after day, when death is so easy to come by. This question, "Why suicide?," is the theme of much that you will encounter in this book. It's operative whenever you hear a person make a suicide threat, because it begs other questions such as "'Why not file for divorce or change jobs or move out of town or visit Disney World or find a new shrink or pray or, even, consider homicide?" You may well know a threatener who rejected the idea of suicide in favor of one of those other options, in which case the question would be "Why not suicide?" (What caused you to reject the idea that led to your threat?). In the end, it amounts to a decision based on what killing oneself could accomplish, as opposed to staying alive.

If we don't know why people reject the suicide option, how can we fully understand their lives? If we don't know the person's reason for living, how can we help him or her to live better? To make a difference, we must know why this person clings to life.

# THE PHILOSOPHICAL QUESTION

We come to the same destination if we start with the question "Why do we die?" To me, that is the ultimate philosophical question, but it is one, ironically, that few philosophers ask. We have professional philosophers, people who make a living "doing philosophy" (their phrase), but most of them avoid this subject because it is either too difficult or too frightening.

Why do we die? What place does dying have in the Grand Design of the universe, and what purpose does it serve? In the context of each reader's religious views, what does dying facilitate

THE MEANING OF LIFE 23

or permit? Nearly every religion holds that death confers entrance to an afterlife, whether Nirvana or the Empyrean, Heaven or Hell. This desired source of reward or deserved source of punishment requires of us only that we die to attain it. So death is necessary to get us to the final chapter, the denouement; it enables us to complete the journey, close the circle. Death, in this view, is not an end but a means, a form of transport from this realm, the false one, to the real world of redemption or damnation.

That's the religious way of seeing it. The more pagan among us see death as a chance to define a life in terms of its worth, up to the moment of death itself. This means that we can "win," have a "meaningful" life, have "given something back" if, at the end, we have done at least one good deed more than bad ones. And death will be a true end of this contest that we have been having with ourselves—no second chance, no "overtime" to right our wrongs and revise the score in our favor one more time. The purpose of *this* death, then, is to force us to examine, daily, what we have accomplished so far. We "take stock," at least subconsciously, and this neverending process of "summing up" is motivated by the always-hovering specter of death. At the end of Goethe's "Faust," he concludes: "The Eternal Feminine leads us ever upward and on." This romantic sentiment has a lovely ring of truth, but I rather think that it is our own mortality that elevates our thoughts and is the source of our striving. So much to prove, so little time.

# III. THE PRINCESS AND THE PRISONER

Here I understand what
they call glory:
the right to love
without limits.

—Inscription on the
gravestone of Albert Camus

The most unnatural act that a human being can perform is suicide. Of course, rape is an unnatural act, but we can to some extent understand the motive for it. To be sure, murder is an unnatural act, but we comprehend that anger can increase to the
point that it drives such an act. Suicide is the most unnatural act
because we strive so mightily to preserve life, to maintain homeostasis, to survive no matter what. In the course of a day, we do
hundreds of things to protect ourselves, hundreds of behaviors
designed for self-enhancement, "supply and maintenance" to keep
the machine running smoothly. For most of us, every waking moment serves the intention of living longer, living better, or, by the
grace of God, both.

Who knows why people try to kill themselves? Naturally, the
experts are dead, but the most likely person to answer this question is someone who has an *acquaintance with death*. People like
this include, among others, those who have had a "near death"
experience, such as a person who has required resuscitation after
cardiac arrest, someone who has emerged from a coma, a near-

drowning victim, someone who has been caught in an avalanche and was nearly buried alive, a person who escaped from a concentration camp, or a soldier or cop who has looked into the barrel of a gun. Although people who have suffered like these definitely qualify as acquaintances of death, each one has, by definition, *defeated* death—has fought back against it to return to the land of the living. They may lack the experience that we seek.

There are people who are knowledgeable about death because they have been compelled to *study* it. These are persons who have received what we call, however insensitively, a "death warrant," for example those who have been singled-out to be killed by a vengeful justice system—the condemned. To a person such as this, a judge may have said something like "I sentence you to be hanged by the neck until you are dead" (in the rather genteel British phrase). Unless some intervention occurs, a man in this circumstance is aptly described as a "dead man walking." He may be in good health, free of pain, clear of mind, and, unlike the terminally ill person, his life is not a burden to him. In short, he has much to live for. He may approach the summing-up of how he feels about life with an immediacy and intensity that is like a flash of inspiration. He may find wisdom in pondering his foreshortened life. Or, he may feel passionately about saving someone else's life before he goes. One such person is described in the fictional story that follows.

In his land, King Bartholomew was loved by many and feared by many, but everyone called him "King Bart." The Queen had died, leaving only his daughter, Katherine, whom everyone loved; with affection, they referred to her simply as "Kate." Twenty years old, she was thought to be the sweetest, kindest young woman in the kingdom, not to mention her beauty. Many likened her to the swan in "Swan Lake," because in her way of walking she seemed to glide above the surface where she walked. For every subject of the kingdom who admired her, another looked on her with envy, because no one had more to live for than did Kate.

Her father, nevertheless, was not without his enemies, and like many ordinary men, his dark side sometimes got the better of him. His reign had survived a series of attempted coups d'etat, and finally, in desperation, the opposition group threatened openly to abduct Kate and hold her hostage. As ransom, they would demand that the King leave his throne and establish a parliamentary democracy. The very thought of someone causing harm to his daughter so outraged King Bart that he had the conspirators locked up and sentenced their leader, the Count Maximilian, to die, as an example to anyone who would in future oppose his authority. Months went by, as King Bart vacillated between his orders to carry out the execution and his reprieves. He was afraid of encouraging some new opposition to rise up against him, but even more afraid to contradict his natural revulsion to capital punishment. Meanwhile, Count Maximilian languished in prison, learning to meet the terrors of solitary confinement with the only counterforce of forgetfulness.

Back at the Palace, King Bart was forced to wrestle with his own *bete noire*: Kate, who had lost her mother only a year before, had just been spurned by her childhood sweetheart, a man called Adam. She told everyone she knew that she had chosen to kill herself. A team of psychiatrists was enlisted to save the royal heir from self-destruction, and a pharmacopeia of remedies was prescribed. Each night, Kate's lady-in-waiting would give her a cupful of anti-depressant pills and, later, Kate would bury them in canisters in her private rose garden, where even the Palace gardeners were forbidden to enter. She well knew that if she took enough of even those harmless pills, she could kill herself; but she reasoned that if she had lived for love until now, she could die for love when the time came.

When Adam remained unmoved by Kate's threat for some time, she became increasingly hostile and isolated; her tantrums were the talk of the kingdom, and even her friends became frightened and found excuses not to visit her. After she had barricaded herself in her chambers for a week, refusing to eat, King Bart became alternately furious and frantic. He knew of no one, not even one of the servants, who could inspire enough confidence in Kate that would bring her to her senses. Desperately, he turned to an old friend and adviser, summoning him from the University one cold midnight.

Professor Wainscoat warmed himself by the fireplace in the King's library, trying to make sense of the story that he was being told about Kate:

WAINSCOAT: I knew her as a girl. She was always so level-headed.

THE KING: No longer, my friend. Since she lost this man, she has taken leave of her senses.

WAINSCOAT: What can I do? I'm a scholar, a man of the cloister. I'm not a worldly man. What do I know of lost love? Indeed, what do I know of love at all? Once I thought I knew the meaning of life itself, but now I'm not so sure.

THE KING: You must help me. Can't you see that I'm losing my daughter? Think of what it means for the kingdom. If I am left without an heir, they will drive me out in favor of another. Please.

WAINSCOAT: That's just like you, your Highness, thinking of yourself first. But neither you nor I can save Princess Kate. What she needs is to listen to someone who knows the meaning of life.

THE KING: What kind of person is that?

WAINSCOAT: She must hear it from a man, because she has been wounded nearly to death by a man. He must have much to gain for himself by helping her. He must have contemplated what life means—to the ends of his endurance and as deeply as the mind can delve. In short, he must be an intelligent man who has made life his constant study.

THE KING: Who, then? Where do we find him?

WAINSCOAT: I'm not talking about a biologist locked in his laboratory, peering at amoebas through a microscope. I'm talking about a man who awakens every morning astonished to be alive, and devotes the rest of the day to figuring out how to make the miracle happen again tomorrow.

THE KING: What kind of person is that? Do you know someone like that?

WAINSCOAT: I've not personally met anyone who fits the description, but I do know where he is and what he is.

THE KING: Where? What?

WAINSCOAT: The answer is simple. Just as a blind man knows everything about trust, the man who knows everything about life is . . . a man condemned to death . . . a man who waits to hear the executioner's voice on Death Row. Think of it: this man knows he will die but not when. Naturally, he *can* answer the question of when merely by killing himself. Every day in that cell, he can think of seventeen ways to end his life. He is a kind of free man, because he can escape whatever his captors are planning for him by a single act of his own— if only he kills himself before they come to get him.

THE KING: Why doesn't he do it?

WAINSCOAT: He doesn't do it because his time, his energy, his mind, must be put to the task at hand: discovering the secret of life. As long as his study requires more time, he *must* live. He is the opposite of a suicidal person.

THE KING: Is there such a man?

WAINSCOAT: I know of one.

THE KING: And what about Kate? Perhaps he could help her.

WAINSCOAT: He could, but now that I come to think of it, her salvation will be won at some cost to you.

THE KING: Anything.

WAINSCOAT: He is Count Maximilian, the man you so vainly sentenced to die, and the one whom you torture by commuting his sentence whenever it's your whim to do so.

THE KING: Maximilian? Never.

WAINSCOAT: Well, goodnight, then.

THE KING: Wait a minute. Why should he help me? What's in it for him?

Wainscoat, preparing to leave, turned around at the door to deliver, with professorial thunder, his closing remark: "You will alter his sentence to read that, as long as his advice to Princess Kate keeps her alive, he will live on. You understand? She dies, he dies. And give him a proper cell, with all the woeful amenities normally given to prisoners of the Crown." Speechless, the King fell back in his chair and stared at the fire.

On reflection, the King realized that he could not force his daughter to cooperate with this effort to save her life, because she seemed so determined to end it. Moreover, the Count would have nothing to do with the idea. When he was approached by the King's friends and told of the Professor's scheme, he said that he would rather die than to do anything to the King's benefit; besides, he had finally adapted to his solitary cell, thank you very much.

Winter wore on, and when Kate told her lady-in-waiting that she had chosen to die on the first day of Spring, the King called on Wainscoat once more for help in this desperate situation.

THE KING: Please. I'm against a wall. What do I do now?

WAINSCOAT: My advice to you is this: know your quarry. The Count is your quarry. Without him, your daughter will not survive this Spring. Find out everything you can about this man. What are his weaknesses? What motivates him? Think of him as an instrument: learn how to play him, to suit your purpose.

King Bart thanked him for his wisdom and set about to find informants in the prison who could secretly observe the Count. They found that the prisoner was writing a book called "The Art of Living." One of the guards was enlisted to take him out of his cell on a pretext, copy pages from the book surreptitiously, replace them and mail the copies, one at a time, to the Princess as though the Count were sending them.

These "letters" from prison were dutifully delivered to Kate, without comment, by her lady-in-waiting. After a few weeks, Kate sent a note to the prison, addressed to the Count. She said she had long harbored feelings of guilt for what her father had done to him, and she was profoundly grateful that he had reached out to her in her dark time. In fact, the thoughts expressed in his words, and only those, were keeping her alive.

Maximilian, quite naturally, was dumbstruck by this note. Who was sending his writings to the Palace? After all, how could he help this lovelorn princess? He soon saw that he was being drawn into a plot by the King to force him into agreeing to his

earlier terms: he must keep the Princess alive or be executed forth-
with. Gradually, his indignation gave way to acceptance and then
to guile. For the sake of his writing, he would enter into this bargain with the Devil—save this girl to save himself. Yet even as he
told himself this rationalization, he realized that the King had
found his weakness after all. He was no enemy of flattery, and after
such a long time of living only for himself, he might be of use to at
least one other person. Besides, he had nothing against the Princess—only her father. He wrote to her sympathetically, she replied
gratefully, and an exchange of notes began.

The Princess survived that Spring, and in fact appeared to be
thriving. One day, tired of receiving her transfusions of spirit by
correspondence, she issued an order to have the Count brought to
her. She would meet him for tea in the parlor of the village hotel.
The first visit went well, although there was heavy surveillance
from men sent by the King, who worried that Kate might be harmed
by the prisoner, or that he would try to escape or both.

Soon, these meetings became routine, occurring at least twice
a month. In good weather, the princess' driver would take them to
a wooded park, where they would walk along a trail for a mile or so
and then retrace the circuit, with several of the King's agents walking discreetly ahead of them by 50 yards, and others following at
a distance behind. Max and Kate spoke softly to each-other, and
from time to time they spoke not at all, alone with their thoughts
and communing with nature.

A year went by. Everyone speculated about what transpired
between these two in their conversations at the hotel or when they
went for a walk. On the only occasion when they were overheard
by the guards, this brief exchange was noted and duly reported
back to the King:

KATE: When all is said and done, I am your hostage.

MAX: Nonsense. You are free to die whenever you want to, if
      that's what you wish to do. If anyone is a hostage, I am the

one. Your life is my life, as long as you want to keep on living.

Now and then, the men heard Max say "Adam" or Kate say "my father." Discussing it among themselves, over a beer at a local pub when the meeting had ended and Max was safely locked up again, the guards could only agree that their charges looked forward to these visits, greeted each-other cordially, and were so engrossed in what they were talking about that they looked surprised when told that it was time for Max to leave. Now and then, they would ask that the time be extended, and the princess would plead so winsomely that the wish was usually granted. Later, Kate would say that the days of these meetings were the happiest of her life.

For his part, the King was well pleased. His daughter seemed to be blossoming and, fortuitously, when word of this "convict counseling" arrangement reached the public, his popularity soared. The King was shown, by the press, to be a man of charity because he had spared a political rival, and compassion because he had sacrificed his principles for the love of his daughter. "Bart the Benevolent," the headlines called him, or "Bart the Magnanimous," or simply "Good King Bart." He was so overwhelmed by pride that he arranged to have a great festival on the Palace grounds. There, with much ceremony, he presented the Order of Merit to Professor Wainscoat, announcing to the multitude that, while it was his own idea to find a counselor to advise Princess Katherine, the first person to agree with him was his old friend Wainscoat. Then Kate appeared on a balcony, every inch a princess in her royal robes and wearing her gleaming tiara. She said nothing, but smiled and waved to the crowd. Everyone could see that she had recovered from the loss of her sweetheart and had made a new start. The King gazed up at her with relief and admiration. At last, he thought, his Kate was ready to begin her apprenticeship to the throne.

One day, disaster struck. An earthquake rocked the kingdom, the first in history. Naturally, the buildings were not safe, nor the roads, and those who escaped the fires were in danger from falling electrical lines. Many died in the brief moments of the temblor, and many more in the chaos that followed. The King was devastated, but he and his court went at once to the scenes of the worst destruction, and Kate offered to help as a nurse. After what seemed like days but was only a few hours, word came that the prison had been heavily hit, and the Count had died there with many fellow inmates. "Every floor came down on the one below," someone said. "He didn't have a chance."

It was months before the fires were put out, the bodies of the dead discovered and buried, and order restored in King Bart's land. Kate moved across these scenes and through these days like a sleepwalker whom no one dared awaken. It was on a crisp morning in January when she found herself seeking out Professor Wainscoat in his rooms at the University. She said "I'm afraid that I am beginning to feel."

WAINSCOAT: That can be dangerous, young lady.

KATE: I ran out of things to do—to help. My father has gone off to some project of rebuilding a dam. For the first time in years, I have no one to talk to.

WAINSCOAT: You can talk to me, of course. But what you must do is talk to your father. That's where the trouble lies. Tell him what has happened in your life. Tell him what the Count meant to you.

KATE: Naturally, you're right. You've always been right. But you must tell *me* one thing. Why did you persuade my father to send Max to me? Why Max?

WAINSCOAT: Even to that you know the answer.

KATE (reflecting): That's so, now that you remind me of it . . .

He was such a brave man. Did you know that the other prisoners named him "Dead Man," and they would call out to him as he walked along the corridor: "Why don't you kill yourself?" "It's easy. I'll tell you how to do it." "What are you afraid of, Dead Man?" He told me that one of the inmates tried to kill him, but he fought back until the guards came. He said "It would have been so easy to let it be. The ordeal would have been over. With all my strength I fought to live." When he said these things to me, I remembered that I had once threatened to die. How could—

WAINSCOAT (interrupting): I see that you have learned a lot from your Max, but now you are mourning him. Go home and grieve his loss. The more you grieve, the more you will understand what he meant to you. Be with your father. Tell him who you are *now*.

At home in the Palace, the princess brooded many days but finally went to her father, accepted a hug from him, and thanked him for bringing the Count into her life. She asked him to walk with her, and took him into his favorite garden, where she knew he would feel tranquil and safe. She told the King that she was going away for a time, to be by herself and think things through.

THE KING: Kate, please. You know I worry about you—even more now that Maximilian is gone.

KATE: Daddy, that's what a father would say.

THE KING: Well, I *am* your father and that's why I say it. I do worry about you. You've had far too many losses already, before you're even grown-up: first your mother, then that Adam, then Max.

KATE: That's my point. I learned everything there is to know when mother died, and when Max died I learned the rest. And since I know all I need to know, I'm leaving.

There was a pause, after which the King, still troubled, asked her where she would go.

KATE: Not far. To the highest mountain I can find and back again.

THE KING: You have my blessing. I truly believe that you will keep yourself safe . . . Tell me, what did the Count—Max— teach you? What did he say that was so profound? Did he question you?

KATE: Not really. He didn't ask me how I felt about something. He told me how *he* felt about things. And what he didn't say was eloquent. He never talked about what it was like in prison, but after he left I would think about what was going on in his mind. I know there were times when he asked himself "What does it mean for me to be here, still breathing? When it ends, what will have been my life's meaning? What is life, that I cling to it so tenaciously?" I know he did, because after a while I asked myself those same questions.

THE KING: How did you answer?

KATE: I figured out that life's first choice is staying alive. I *chose* life. Sometimes, when I awake in the morning, I say to my- self "Live today. Live today. Live today."

THE KING: There was a time when the will to live was not so strong in you. I thought you wanted to kill yourself be- cause of Adam.

KATE: I am staying alive in spite of him.

THE KING: Then I thought you wanted to kill yourself because of me.

KATE: I am staying alive because of you.

THE KING: And Max?

KATE: He is Life.

As the years went by, Kate walked many mountains and came back many times to the Palace, bringing much joy to her father and reassurance to the people of the land. When King Bart died peacefully in his sleep, Kate became the very model of a Queen, ruling her people with a grace born of much sorrow. Moral: the best person to keep someone alive is a person who reveres life.

# IV. A BARGAIN WITH DEATH

> Much of the Egyptian religion remains a mystery to us. It is full of contradictions, inexplicable rituals, and impenetrable texts. Amid the complexity, one simple fact stands out: it was a great human bargain with death. Almost everything that ancient Egypt has left us—the pyramids, the tombs, the temples—represents an attempt to overcome that awful mystery at the center of all our lives.
>
> —Douglas Preston,
> "All the King's Sons"

At the close of the day, most of us can take pride in a victory of choice: as did the Princess, we have chosen to live. If we are frank, we believe that life is worth the struggle, and we plan to go on living as long as that course is open to us. In short, each of us affirms life.

Right now, there are those among us who will deny themselves that affirmation. The tragedy of suicide is recorded through all history of the acts of Man. From Plato, we learn of the Greek "'law" that condemned to ignominious burial each person who killed himself or herself out of weakness or cowardice. The Stoics reversed this view, allowing even the questionable suicide to be congratulated for having followed out the potentialities of Nature. And the Roman sage, Cicero, provided us with the cautionary tale of Hegesias of Cyrene, who argued for suicide as a rational act; sadly, the doctrine of Hegesias spread throughout Egypt, where people took to killing themselves in such numbers that its founder was banished. Not much is lost, in the history of ideas, from the belief of Hegesias to that of the French writer Montaigne, who wrote that "the most voluntary death is the finest." If people took that value judgment to heart, there would be many more suicides than we could bear.

How much suicide can we bear? Some would say that Twenty-First Century men and women are much more civilized than their counterparts in ancient times, because the suicide rate in America stays at about 30,000, year after year. You can think of that as a small number if you compare it to the size of a good weekend crowd at a pro baseball game. Even so, the total would represent the entire population of a small American city. And when you realize that, on an average day, 82 people die by this means who would otherwise have lived—more than three each hour who die for no good reason—you will agree that this is a social problem worth solving. So many deaths like this are brought home to us, when they occur, by newspapers and television because they do shock us, and because it does concern us as human beings. Collectively, we say to ourselves "What a waste."

## DON'T KILL YOURSELF

Zero is the first number in the number series. The Zero Commandment is the one that was left off Moses' list: don't kill yourself. The prophet who wrote Genesis did not include, in the story of the Mosaic tablets, "Thou shalt not end thy life for any purpose," because it must have seemed obvious that God would have none of it.

The wrath of God notwithstanding, as Americans living in this violent place and time, you and I are more likely to kill ourselves (one person in 67) than be murdered (one person in 99). How can that be possible? Was that The Enemy we met in the mirror this morning? Another way to look at it is this: ask yourself "Who can kill me?" This graphic answers the question for you.

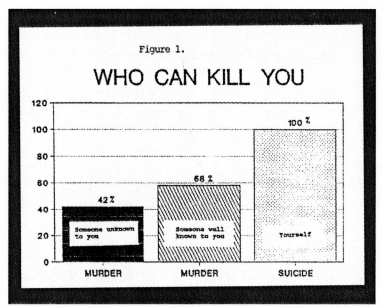

Figure 1.

# WHO CAN KILL YOU

This shows that a stranger could be your enemy, but it's more likely that a friend or relative or acquaintance might be your enemy. The worst potential enemy is *you*.

Thank your stars that we *can* kill ourselves. Knowing that reminds us how mortal we are. Even though we die daily, there are days when we are not in mortal danger, and thus we might forget. Let's face it, each day we make the choice of our death or Nature's. Alone among the animals are we aware that we can destroy the one gift we never deserved—the gift of life.

Suicide is the leading absurd cause of death. And because death is by itself absurd, suicide merely compounds the fault. To act absurdly mocks evolution. In the Twenty-first Century, we have come to believe that human beings can change themselves in certain ways—for example through genetic engineering—that have nothing to do with survival of the fittest. Any change that is produced by these means must be a result of rational deliberation; that is the civilized way. And one measure of civilization is the difference between the damage we can do and what we don't.

This is a book about the basest human action, base because it causes suffering intentionally, base because it leaves a legacy of senseless rage. Suicide is more heinous than murder, for it is the one crime that can have no earthly retribution. I do not take up this subject lightly. It is inexorably grim. I have many times put it aside because of its repugnance. One thought that kept me going is a famous maxim of the French *enfant terrible*, Serge Gainsbourg, who said "Ugly is better than beautiful, because ugly lasts longer." We tend to feel that way about many ills, that they have always plagued mankind and always will. Even so, there is much to be said for expanding our range of vision to ask a question such as: "What would life be like if no one committed suicide?" From this sort of speculation came, for instance, the recent discovery of a link between common bacteria and peptic ulcer. For many years, this debilitating and potentially fatal condition was routinely given the psychiatric diagnosis of "psychosomatic disorder." ("No physical ailment has ever been more closely tied to psychological turbulence.")[1] But, if the cause is bacterial, the cure is not psychotherapy or Valium: it is one of the antibiotics. This development led a prominent scientist to say that "Over time, within perhaps even my lifetime, we should be able to eliminate ulcer disease from the human race."[2] This demonstrates the utility of the "paradigm shift," in which redefining a problem opens the way to its solution.[3]

A similar example concerns the heinous crime of rape. Only in recent years have we come to understand that rape expresses a psychopathic urge for power, not for sex—not for conquest but control. This insight now appears obvious to most people, but it was not the prevailing view twenty-five years ago.[4] As a "defining

[1] "Marshall's Hunch," by Terrence Monmaney, *The New Yorker*, September 20, 1993, 64-72, p.64.

[2] *Ibid.*, p. 69.

[3] The principle is that if you want to explain X, you must look in a different place for the cause, from the place where you've looked until now.

[4] For example, in 1975 no state in the Union made it a crime for a husband to rape his wife. As a California State Senator, Bob Wilson, put it, "If you can't rape your wife, who can you rape?"

concept," this new way of interpreting the pathology of the rapist has enormous practical value: for example, when a police detective is trying to create the profile of a serial rapist, the focus can be placed not on a man who desires women, but one who has a grudge against them. In short, a rapist is not a "sex fiend" but a woman-hater.

What would life be like if no one committed rape? The point is that we needn't have ugliness like that forever. We can do something about it now. The only saving grace in studying suicide is that knowledge is power: if we know enough about it, it can be excised from the human condition. So it was with the keeping of slaves and the belief in a geocentric universe.

## A WILLED TRAGEDY

Let's be clear about what type of suicide we are discussing here. Everyone knows an elderly person who, overwhelmed by the pain and degradation of the body collapsing around the soul, says things like "I might as well be dead" or "Maybe you should put me out of my misery," or, as the situation worsens, "I want to die." Even though, when we hear them, we find these laments chilling, we can empathize with them because we know that there might come a time when we would feel the same way. And whether these people who protest of wanting to die are serious or not, we understand if they don't appreciate our efforts to keep them alive. After all, when one is terminally ill, every second thought is of suicide. Even Sigmund Freud, a man capable of the clearest logical thinking, hastened his own death by asking his doctor to give him an extra dose of morphine, to escape the pain of cancer of the jaw.

People kill themselves for the best and worst of reasons. The person who suffers from AIDS sees his body become helpless to protect itself against infection, and knows that his days are numbered. The religious fanatic believes that he or she will be welcome in Heaven and wants to get there as soon as possible. The risk-taker takes one risk too many. Romeo killed himself because he thought that Juliet was dead, and Juliet killed herself because he killed himself. Whether for stupidity or salvation, by accident or to gain one last measure of control over an oppressive body, people take their own lives as the lesser of evils. Because we can see that they have chosen between two almost equally feared alternatives, we accept that they have not really made a choice at all. All things considered, they *had* to die in this way, at this time. I call this *involuntary* suicide.

*Voluntary* suicide is another matter. It is death for *every wrong reason*. It is a highly motivated crime, planned with malice aforethought. It is willed and has a purpose. It destroys, at a minimum, two human lives (as revealed in later chapters of this book). What the suicidal person accomplishes by willing his or her death is by no means a trivial result: the person takes control of death, uses it, shapes it into an instrument that can carry out a task. This is not a suicide of the extra dose of morphine or driving too fast on a mountain road or calling in Dr. Kevorkian (of whom more later). This is not the "cry for help" of a person who knows that he or she will be rescued in time. Those who kill themselves voluntarily do not flirt with death; they court it brazenly, lusting for their own blood.

This book intends to show you that suicide is:

- crime without punishment
- death without honor
- a mockery of life
- the courage of cruelty
- a fraud against Nature

This is no laughing matter. Each person who has seriously thought of suicide knows what I mean. As will be made clear in the chapters to follow, this kind of death is by no means the rapture of religious fantasy and far from the final exaltation of romantic love. This is the suicide of gun barrel in the mouth, razor blade at the wrist, a get-down-on-the-tracks invocation of the Angel of Death.

Others have written about the suicides of poets. I am writing about the suicides of monsters.

They say the human heart starts beating at the moment of conception, and this phenomenon is a metaphor for the life to follow, because the heart begins its journey long before there is a working brain. How can that vital force dissolve itself? How could a miracle of creation in the womb be undone by its own invention? How could God's hand, reaching out to Adam with the divine spark in Michelangelo's painting, be thrust aside? I seek to do battle with the terror that is suicide, to best it in combat, and to lay its ghost.

# V. WHY PEOPLE KILL
# THEMSELVES

If suicide is allowed
> then everything is allowed.
If anything is not allowed
> then suicide is not allowed.
This throws a light on the nature of ethics,
> for suicide is, so to speak,
> the elementary sin.
And when one investigates it,
> it is like investigating mercury vapour
> in order to comprehend the nature of vapours.

> —Ludwig Wittgenstein, who
> lost three brothers to suicide,
> *Notebooks 1914-1916*

There are those whom we have loved very deeply, who reveal their true selves to us only after love has died. It's like this with suicides, whom we only know after the fact. As the time approaches for the final act, they are out of touch with us, preferring to dwell on their quest without interruption. Imagine the solitude of a suicidal person before the act. This person must hide out, avoid the others who would intervene to keep him or her alive. If people were to intrude on this isolation, they probably would be repelled by the sight and keep on going, as would a cautious person fear to touch a leper. This is a true story about a man who will be called "Leo" here:

> Neighbors had come to notice that [Leo] seemed withdrawn
> and disengaged lately. He could often be seen through an
> open garage door sitting alone in a chair—his head bowed
> between his knees as his two children played with each
> other only a few feet away in the neatly manicured front
> yard. Sometimes, one neighbor said, [Leo] would sit by
> himself in his car, his head drooped against the steering
> wheel—a picture of dejection.

(San Jose *Mercury News*, May 1, 1997, p. 4B.)

When his wife returned home from working late one night, she
found Leo and their two children, ages 5 and 9, dead in the bath-
tub; as far as is known, the father had drowned the children, taken
an overdose of his anti-depressant medication, and drowned himself.

Later, a person who knew the family said: "I'm so sorry to see
those young children had to die. I hope the bastard rots in hell."
Most of us will share that sentiment, but even though we haven't
a shred of sympathy for Leo, we can find meaning in these events.
The newspaper article gave us a vivid word picture of a man ap-
proaching the end of his tether. He sat in the garage or in his car,
thinking, wondering, weighing, calculating, plotting, alternately
embracing and scorning the Life Force. These thoughts occur within
the "silence of the heart" where, for Camus, the suicidal plan is
conceived. It's then that the knife-wielding hand measures the
throat for size, or the gun is tested to see how much force the
trigger needs. This is when the pills are counted to make sure
there are enough to kill.

In the case of Leo, baby-killer, what could have caused him to
do this despicable act? What could have doomed Leo, an ordinary
man, to such a fate as suicide? The answer lies in the relationship
that Leo had with his wife. Think what a sight greeted her when
she saw her husband and her only children squeezed together,

floating in the water of a tub. When the water drained, her life went with it.

A tragic case like this, with the headline 'DESPONDENT' MAN, 2 CHILDREN FOUND DEAD IN FAMILY'S BATH-TUB is the kind of story that appears regularly in the newspapers of any urban area. Without belittling the agony of the surviving wife, events such as these are commonplace in our culture, and when we are through feeling sympathy our very human response is to try to make sense of them. Why did Leo decide to solve his problem in this way? For that matter, why did Socrates or Cleopatra or Ernest Hemingway or Vincent Van Gogh? For a multitude of reasons, you may say, but it is not beyond possibility that the many reasons behind each of those suicides have one common denominator. Let's see if we can find it.

Before doing that, let's turn the coin over to its other side, and consider a situation in which people decide *not* to kill themselves. Imagine that you are a refugee from Rwanda who has fled the civil war that rages there, to Zaire to save your life. The difficulty is that you are not welcome in Zaire, and there is no food for you and no way for you to get food. You are starving to death. We who live in affluence have no reference-point to the word "starve," because it is as far from our existence as the ability to fly. About as close as we come to the feeling of starvation is if we are required by the doctor to have a blood test for cholesterol and must fast for twelve hours beforehand. If you've done this, you know how your body feels in the tenth or eleventh hour. The feeling is so foreign to our normal way of feeling that we can scarcely describe it, but it is a force of Nature, and we are hard-pressed to put it out of mind.

The real starvation of the real Rwandan refugees means that their bodies are dissolving around them: the term "wasting away" refers to the catabolic process by which an organism literally eats itself to death. The worst images, of course, are of the children, lying on their sides, reaching up in supplication to the forgiving angel they know will never come. We turn off the TV set and try to forget.

Why don't the adult refugees kill themselves, if only to leave the food that they might have eaten for their children? Why don't they kill the children to spare them excruciating pain, when they know that no miraculous rescue is coming? Why do they not kill the children *and* themselves (as did Leo, the "bastard" who should rot in hell)? They don't because they can't; they can't because they don't have the reason for it that Leo had. Of course, there are suicides among the refugees of Rwanda, but far fewer than one would expect. From our own well-fed perspective, it would be foolish not to do it. But they don't because, in their minds, doing it would be foolish. The Life Force grips them tightly, and they accept every chance or sign of staying alive.

Every day, millions of people who are the victims of intolerable circumstances suffer on without killing themselves. For most, the idea of suicide never comes to them. Think of a mother who has just lost a child in an auto accident; think of a wife whose husband of 40 years has just died, or a man whose lifelong business enterprise has ended in bankruptcy. Viktor Frankl, the psychiatrist who survived two concentration camps in World War II and wrote about his experiences, observed that " . . . it is a well-known empirical fact that in times of war and crises the number of suicides decreases."[5] During the Battle of Britain, when London was bombed almost every night, the rates of both suicide and homicide actually declined. And, contrary to legend, there was no epidemic of suicides in New York following the stock market crash of 1929.

Neither ruin nor disaster, nor terror nor suffering a loss causes people to kill themselves. Feelings such as those events create may well occur to the refugee from Rwanda at least once an hour. By any definition of the word "despair," we could believe that it describes that person's state of mind. But this man or woman keeps on keeping on. Why? They lack *the reason* for killing themselves. A critical element in the equation is missing: they don't have a motive for the crime.

[5] Frankl, Viktor. *Psychotherapy and Existentialism*. New York: Clarion, 1967, p. 116.

# THE REASON

Most media accounts of a suicide would not be complete without referring to the deceased as having recently been "depressed" or "despondent." This is a good example of the explanation of a phenomenon that has outstripped its usefulness. It is repeated by rote, on the well-meaning assumption that it adds to our understanding of what has happened. We fervently want to understand it when someone is self-destructive, because it shakes our feeling of intactness and challenges our faith in the rightness of things. The word "depression" sounds so apt because it connotes a kind of sinking or diminishing of the person, dragging him or her down and down until death is the only option. Apart from that metaphor, the concept of depression is an attractive one because so much has been heard about it recently that it has become largely the malady of our times—as "anxiety" was the watchword for emotional distress in the 50s and 60s. Depression is believed to be suffered by so many people in Western nations these days, that producing the drug Prozac became a billion-dollar industry in the 90s.[6]

The rise in popularity of depression as a mental disease notwithstanding, it is irrelevant to our topic here. We want to know what causes suicide, and it turns out that the part played by depression is negligible. The founder of the field of Suicidology, Edwin Shneidman, recently summed up the results of 40 years of study on this subject, when he wrote "Depression *never* causes suicide." In denying that there is a causal link between suicide and depression, Shneidman implied that antidepressant drugs are powerless to prevent people from killing themselves; they may be profoundly

---

[6] A newspaper reports that "Visits in which depression was diagnosed almost doubled over the 10 years [1985-1994], from about 11 million to more than 20.4 million...researchers said." (San Francisco *Chronicle*, February 18, 1998). Did the American people become twice as depressed during that decade, or did the diagnosis become fashionable?

beneficial in alleviating depressive states, but they cannot be expected to reduce the suicide rate.[7]

Depression and the suicidal motive have one common element: anger. The dynamic force that fuels depression is anger that has no focus and can find no outlet. For most people, anger is released in brief bursts of temper; it is most often directed toward the person(s) who caused the angry feelings, but it's well known that anger is sometimes expressed toward the family cat or a convenient wall. But imagine a person who cannot release anger in these or any other effective ways. Think of that person as being surrounded by a plexiglass cylinder: anger expressed outward is deflected back inside. As a result, the angry feelings that were felt toward someone else are now felt within. The person hates himself or herself.

Anyone who has visited a mental hospital where people are kept for long periods of time, and some remain until they die, will have seen the "outer limits" of depression. In the back wards where these unfortunate men and women are "housed," they sit for long hours in isolation, crying uncontrollably; when someone comes near, they say things like "I'm no good" or "I am no use to anybody. Why don't you take me out and shoot me?" These are the ramblings of the severely depressed, and they show how anger raised to the nth power becomes rage. But even rage so vicious and all-pervasive as this is not the prelude to suicide in these people: very few back-ward depressives kill themselves; most wail on in their dismal rooms, festering in self-loathing. The real targets of their fury never know it, and escape its force.

This description of the hospitalized depressive will remind the reader of Leo, who sat in his garage with his head bowed. No doubt Leo, at one stage, *was* seriously depressed, but something happened to him: he turned a corner, made a transition to a differ-

---

[7] A cartoon in a recent *New Yorker* magazine shows how firmly the connection between suicide and depression is imbedded in public consciousness. It's a drawing of a rat who has hanged himself in his cage. A man in a white coat tells another: "Discouraging data on the antidepressant."

ent mode of expressing his anger. He chose suicide. His anger, escalating to rage at some critical moment, was now free for *outward* expression. The drowning of his children was part of the fallout from this volcanic eruption.

We have seen that the rage of a suicidal person is qualitatively different from the rage that feeds depression. Now, what purpose does the choice of suicide serve? The answer to what a suicidal person wishes to accomplish lies in what we observe that suicide *does* accomplish. In this approach, we can work back from the effect of an event to identify its cause. As an example, if we came across a farmhouse in Kansas that has been torn apart and smashed to the ground, with the terrified owners cowering in a storm cellar, the high-probability inference would be that a tornado had passed by. Similarly, what suicide does can help us to identify what suicide is.

## THE MESSAGE

If you have known someone who committed suicide, or even if your closest encounter with an act like this comes from reading a newspaper account of it, you will recall that the death occurred in the context of a relationship (Very few hermits kill themselves, and even so there are very few hermits who are completely cut off from human ties.). Therefore, virtually everyone who kills himself or herself leaves someone behind among the living. If we were to watch this discarded person carefully, we could see that, in most cases, he or she is devastated by the experience. After the initial shock of learning about the event, this person will run the gauntlet of negative emotions, from denial to humiliation to self-blame (We shall meet a survivor of suicide, up close and personal, in a later chapter of this book.). If this is what suicide produces, then it must have been what the suicidal person intended.

Any relationship ends with the death of one partner, but when the death is suicidal, our ordinary understanding of what death means is turned inside-out. A death that occurs willfully is chosen for the *purpose* of ending a relationship. Suicide is a means by which the one who dies sends a message to the one who lives. On the surface, the message might be as harmless as "You won't have me to kick around anymore." But because we know that most suicides do serious harm to survivors, there must be more meaning in this message.

By killing himself or herself, a person makes a statement more profound than words could express; it means:

1. You are not worth living for;
2. You are the cause of my troubles, the source of my misery;
3. You have driven me to do this.

Here is anger that was not turned back onto the self (as in depression), but could never be given voice while the person was alive. The survivor is told: I could not continue living *because of you.*

A rage so corrosive could only have been manufactured in a relationship so poisoned that one person is willing to die to end it. This is the bargain referred to above, a bargain with death that permits one person to sacrifice his or her life in order to find victory in death itself. The "victory" consists in trading a life for a life, because the person who survives will live on in misery.

After a suicide occurs, the natural reaction of people who knew the dead person is to ask "what for?," "why?," "Who is responsible?" This is a normal defensive reaction because we cannot tolerate this amount of ambiguity, and because our feeling of security is threatened by a death that makes no sense. The primitive impulse to assign blame will, in most instances, find a scapegoat: some person will be charged with major responsibility for the death. That person, who could be called the "intended victim" of the suicidal act, is very likely the person whose relationship with the suicide was most malignant.

The identity of an intended victim is often made obvious to the other survivors by means of a process of "marking." The right words said to the right person will serve this purpose, or the circumstances of the death itself will make the lethal intention perfectly clear; in by far the majority of cases, no note will be required to do this marking. Because others need to fix blame, a person so marked has become the "target" of someone else's death. There is seldom doubt about who it is and, as will be shown in a later chapter by the case of Dr. Chance, he or she probably knows before anyone else.

People kill themselves because they want to punish another person and cannot figure out how to do it short of taking their own lives. They are filled with hatred toward at least one other person and have no other means to express their anger. They want to kill the other person(s) (There could be more than one.), but they cannot—for numerous reasons. The next best thing to killing that person is to destroy his or her life. A person's life can be destroyed by branding that person as a "murderer," who will carry the stigma forever in the eyes of others. As long as he or she lives, the murderer must bear a guilt that comes both from outside and within. This fate may be worse than death itself. The suicide trades his or her own death for the other person's living death. It's worth the bargain. The act of suicide is an act of spite.

# DOCTOR DEATH

You may have wondered why seemingly rational people call in the infamous Dr. Kevorkian to "assist" them in committing suicide. On the videotapes that they made before they died, some of these folks sounded perfectly logical in explaining what they had chosen to do. It occurred to me that, if they were competent enough to understand what was about to happen and sign an official form giving Kevorkian their consent, they were competent enough to kill themselves on their own—that is, without assistance. Something else must be going on in these cases.

Just as the Rwandan mother does not commit suicide because she lacks the motive (She doesn't hate anyone.), the person who calls Kevorkian does not *want* to commit suicide. For sure, he or she wants to die, but by committing suicide someone might be blamed for it. Since the person hates no one, an innocent survivor could be branded a murderer by this death. The next best thing is to ask Kevorkian to play the role of murderer. If he kills the person, no one will be blamed but Kevorkian, and he doesn't care. Even though most life-embracing people find it offensive, this is the perfect solution to a terrible dilemma for those who want to die but cannot bring themselves to take the involuntary suicide way out. Whether the Kevorkian Solution is branded as homicide or euthanasia has no bearing on the subject of this book. It has nothing to do with suicide.

# VI. A HAPPY DEATH

We are in the power of
nothing when once we have
death in our own power.

—Seneca, an exemplar of the involuntary suicide, who killed
himself when ordered to do so by the emperor Nero
*Epistulae morales*

Anyone who would understand suicide must know a few things
about death. Consider the power of death: *it* claims *us*. Every he-
donistic act that we perform, every step taken toward stability,
homeostasis, the Golden Mean, is like a defiant fist being thrust in
the face of death. We speak of "cheating" death, as though it
were our opponent in a game of cards. The poet Dylan Thomas
tells us to "rage" against death—as if it would pay attention. Most
of us will never catch the eye of death as it levels us, with its scythe,
like so much wheat. But the suicidal person wants to confront
death head-on and take control, feeling that he or she is better
than death, because only he or she knows *how* or *when*.

This sounds abstract and philosophical, but in practical terms
it can lead to thoughts like these: if I choose the time and place
and means of death, it's my death, not cancer's. In fact, this reasoning justifies many an involuntary suicide, as described in Chapter
IV. The poor souls of the Heaven's Gate commune in San Diego
suffered from a group delusion; but at least they knew that, when
it came to dying, they were in charge.

The *voluntary* suicide is guided by logic like this:

1. I have a problem;
2. The problem is unsolvable;
3. I am willing to pay any price;
4. I shall die anyway;
5. My life belongs to me;
6. A person uses what he or she has available;
7. My life can be a weapon;
8. To cause a death is a moral crime;
9. The punishment for causing a death is lifelong;
10. The problem will be solved when I place the *blame* for causing my death on the right person.

This theme of discovering the utility of death was a source of fascination to Camus, whose first novel *La Mort Heureuse*, describes a "happy death." The hero's final moments are a time of resignation when, in the last lines of the book: "A stone among stones, he returned, in the joy of his heart, to the truth of the unmoving worlds."[8] Because we die, life is absurd—unless: unless our death can serve a *purpose*. That is what every great martyr, from Joan of Arc to Lincoln to Martin Luther King to Gandhi, has understood.

This concept of making your death a masterpiece occurs, at least subconsciously, to even the most dimly perceptive of suicidal people. Remember that the two essential ingredients for suicide are (1) a relationship and (2) anger. In review, something has gone wrong in a relationship, and one of the partners is angry enough to kill. So even as it answers the trivial question "When will I die?," suicide answers the more compelling question "'How can I kill?'"

## THE TARGET

X hates Y. Frustrated in his or her efforts to kill Y, or even to vent rage toward Y in any satisfying way, X wallows in disappointment. This self-directed anger may manifest itself in the symptoms of depression—at least in the eyes of anyone who observes X writh-

[8] From Murphy, P. (1982) *Camus*. New York: Random House, p. 142.

ing in consternation. As we have seen, this depression is only a *sign* that suicide might occur, not a reason for its occurring. The next step for X, which most people would never even consider, is the silent resolve to express this hatred through suicide. To see how this process works itself out in actual practice, we can adopt the viewpoint of a helicopter hovering above the scene of a suicide drama, videotaping it from the moment when the plan first begins to take shape, through the event itself, and further to record its aftermath. Later, replaying the tape, we can see how, when, and where, and ultimately determine why. The most critical intelligence, however, is finding out *who*.

After a suicide, a mystery plot is set in motion. As in the conventional murder mystery, we know who has died, but in this mystery we must discover who the *other* victim was. To do that, we search among the dead person's relationships to find out the one that was the most defective, toxic, potentially dangerous. When we identify this relationship, we know the identity of the person who was meant to suffer from this death. There may be many who suffer, but usually one will be held responsible for the death and will bear the most blame. This is the *target* of suicide.

A target is likely to be found among those who have been connected to the suicidal person by some intense bond or tie. Examples are:

1. a bullying or abusive father;
2. an overprotective, smothering mother;
3. an absent or abandoning parent;
4. a scornful spouse;
5. a rejecting lover;
6. an envied sibling;
7. a punitive boss;
8. a destructive critic;
9. a predator, such as a rapist or murderer;
10. a betrayer, such as a rival who reveals secrets.

In every suicide story will be found one actor such as these, because antagonists play a part in every life.

The challenge in the art of explaining a suicide is to find, among the prime suspects, a principal target. It may be more than one of those adversaries listed above; it could be a group or institution or organization. (A real-life example of the latter is presented later in this chapter.). It could also be the memory of someone who is dead or no longer present in the suicidal person's life; in short, a "ghost." The key criterion, from the standpoint of the suicide's thinking, is that the other person or persons or group or entity or ghost must be *punished* for some reason.

How could there be so much animosity between people that one thinks of dying just to punish the other? Let's look at an example, so commonplace in contemporary life that nearly everyone will know someone whose story this could be. Paul and Elizabeth are getting a divorce after fourteen years of a stormy marriage. Their children, Stevie and Emily, are ten and eight respectively. The lawyers for each parent are trying to work out a financial agreement and, at least in the beginning, Elizabeth and Paul are trying to cohabit for the children's sake.

Paul is an engineer who works for the Public Works Department of a large city. His pension will be a considerable sum when he retires, and when her lawyer brings it to her attention, Elizabeth wants a share. She gave him the best years of her adult life, and she wants a cash settlement if only to help put the children through college. Her assumption is that primary custody of the children will be awarded to her; she expects that their normal residence will be with her in the family house, and that they can visit Paul on weekends and for a week or two in the summer. For his part, Paul feels that because he earned every penny of the pension money, every penny should be his; besides, he intends to remarry and start a new family, and he wants to be able to promise them a secure retirement. Because Elizabeth has no job, he thinks she will be well provided-for by alimony, as well as child support until the children are eighteen.

In many a divorce, a conflict can be alleviated by compromise until some issue rubs two attorneys together, igniting a blaze. As a result of their differences over the pension, Paul and Elizabeth clash about her offered buyout of his equity in the house. Soon, two people who once thought alike on everything—long, long ago—can find no common ground on anything. Sound familiar?

Elizabeth and Paul become so antagonistic to each-other that, eventually, the handing-over of children from one to the other resembles the exchanges at Checkpoint Charlie on the edge of East Berlin in the Cold War. The mother takes them to the parking lot of a fast-food restaurant and watches them enter, while the father enters from another direction and joins them at a table. This charade of the dysfunctional non-family is taken in stride by most parents, but for Paul and Elizabeth it is only the end of Act One of their tragedy.

Elizabeth reveals that she has found a new lover, Sam. She will be including this man in outings with the children, and already Stevie says he thinks that Sam is "cool." This simple statement will be recalled, later on, as the point when the deconstruction of Paul's ego began. After a series of pitched battles over small concessions have been lost, Paul begins to feel that, just as all men are created equal, all ex-husbands are equally pathetic. He becomes sullen, withdrawn, and even his lawyer has trouble in communicating with him.

For her part, Elizabeth is radiantly happy; her new affair has increased her energy level and her confidence as well. What used to be reviled as adultery has actually strengthened her hand in this chess game, because the children are becoming more vocal about their preference for being with her and Sam instead of morose old Daddy. Paul, desperate for answers, begins a weak campaign to have the children enrolled in counseling; he has read about "parent alienation syndrome"[1] in a magazine article suggested by the

---

[1] A situation in which one parent manipulates a child into believing that the other parent is uncaring or unworthy. Experts have likened this process to brainwashing.

attorney, and has cast himself in the role of potential victim. In his mind, he has lost his wife to another man, and may eventually lose his children's regard and affection.

One day Paul takes the kids to the beach. It's hot, and the three of them are wearing shorts. Stevie has taken off his shirt and Emily is wearing a halter. Paul falls asleep on the sand, and awakens to the sound of the children fighting; they are wrestling in a clump of bushes nearby. To his dismay, Paul realizes that they are rolling about in poison ivy. He orders them to rinse off the sand in the water and then hustles them home. When they arrive, he puts them in separate showers and tells them to wash thoroughly with soap. While overseeing Stevie's shower, he realizes that the boy cannot clean the middle of his back, so he reaches in with a washcloth to help. Then he goes around to the other shower and helps Emily wash her back as well. A few days later, Emily tells her counselor about this incident and the counselor, ever alert for wrongdoing, asks "How did you feel when Daddy washed your back?" When Emily answers "funny," the counselor reaches for the phone and makes a report of suspected abuse to the local social services agency. With this, the second act of the story of Elizabeth and Paul comes to a close: thunder and curtain fall.

Events move swiftly from now on. Paul is taken to police headquarters and questioned; he angrily denies the charge of touching his daughter inappropriately. Because they are constitutionally suspicious and because they don't know whom to believe, the police send a woman officer to interview Emily in her home. By now, everyone involved is confused and angry; no one knows what to do, but there is a nagging feeling that something should be done. The police are unable to make up their minds between the conflicting stories and drop the case. Elizabeth, however, believes that *something* happened, and that it is her maternal duty to prevent anything worse in future. She asks her attorney to persuade the judge to order that the visitation between Emily and her father be supervised by a social worker. Paul realizes that a moment's poor judgment may now have cost him the right to have visits with his daughter as they were before. He asks his attorney to persuade the judge to order a full-scale evaluation of the family, involving psychological testing of himself and Elizabeth to see who is the more "fit" parent, and of Stevie and Emily to find out if they have been damaged in some way by the current conflict.

What Paul could not foresee is that, because of his indignation at having been accused of incestuous feelings toward his daughter, he has reached for a double-edged sword. When the results of the evaluation are announced, he finds that he is diagnosed as having a "personality disorder"; Elizabeth is labeled as "dependent," and the children are found to suffer from "marked anxiety"—not surprisingly, considering the turmoil that their parents have created in their lives. With labels like these in their files, it is likely that this family will be trapped in "the system" for years to come, and find themselves in many a courtroom.

The reader can imagine various possible scripts for the saga of the lives of Paul and Elizabeth, from love to commitment to parenthood to estrangement to hostility to war and, perhaps, eventually to a truce and mutual respect. They, after all, are imaginary people. Real people are, sometimes, not so lucky, as the newspaper account shown in Figure 2 reminds us.

## Figure 2[1]

# Author Michael Dorris Commits Suicide

**His book spotlighted fetal alcohol syndrome**

*Chronicle News Services*

Manchester, N.H.

Last Friday, the day he was scheduled to speak at a conference celebrating the 25th anniversary of the Native American Studies department he founded at Dartmouth College, author Michael Dorris checked into a motel in Concord, N.H., under an assumed name and, according to police, put a plastic bag over his head and committed suicide.

Dorris was an acclaimed novelist, seemingly at the top of his game. He penned novels for adults and children, essays, short stories and nonfiction. His novel "A Yellow Raft on Blue Water" has sold hundreds of thousands of copies.

But he is perhaps best known for having brought the problem of fetal alcohol syndrome into the national limelight with "The Broken Cord." In the early '70s, Dorris, whose father belonged to the Modoc tribe, was widely credited with being the first single father in the country to adopt. The child was a Native American suffering from fetal alcohol syndrome.

The autobiographical book, which was

Michael Dorris had been going through a difficult divorce battle and had attempted suicide once before

*BY MICHAEL MACOR THE CHRONICLE*

about his adopted son, Abel, won the National Book Critics Circle Award in 1989. It also became a hit TV movie.

The story, however, ended in tragedy: The son was killed at age 23 when he was hit by a car while walking along a road. Dorris later adopted two more children, both also with fetal alcohol syndrome.

Although friends and colleagues were stunned by the news of Dorris' suicide, there was some indication that Dorris had been troubled in recent weeks. Dorris, 52, was involved in a difficult divorce battle with his wife, Louise Erdrich, also an award-winning novelist, with whom he had had a close working partnership.

Friends said Dorris had first tried to kill himself on Good Friday, but had been discov-

ered. He was then hospitalized for a short time for "exhaustion." Last Friday, Dorris was reported missing by the Brattleboro Retreat, a Vermont psychiatric hospital, according to Brattleboro Police.

Concord Police Lieutenant Paul Murphy said Dorris left a note with "instructions to whoever found him, which happened to be us." He would not elaborate.

The apparently acrimonious divorce "devastated" Dorris, his publisher, Bill Shinker, said. "Who wouldn't be, in that situation? It's a natural reaction."

The divorce was not Dorris' idea, friends said. His last novel, published in January, bore a dedication that he could have changed had he wished. "For Louise," it says. "Who found the song and gave me voice."

Erdrich issued the following statement yesterday through the office of the couple's friend and literary agent Charles "Cy" Rembar of New York. "Michael did a great deal of good for the world. He is deeply grieved by his family and friends."

At one time, the couple's relationship was described as idyllic. They met in 1972 at Dartmouth and married nine years later. The two were mutual supporters, editors and collaborators. Erdrich dedicated her novel "The Beet Queen" to Dorris with these words: "To Michael. Complice in every word, essential as air."

Later stories revealed that Dorris and his wife, Erdrich,[2] were also involved in a game of bluff and challenge, with their children as pawns. Shortly before he killed himself, the police began an investigation into an allegation of sexual abuse by Dorris involving "one or more children." He told a friend "My life is over." Apparently, no one was able to decipher this message, and by the time he registered in the motel under an assumed name, plastic bag in hand, "all the King's horses and all the King's men" could not have saved him. One reason for this book is to sensitize concerned friends (not to mention social workers and lawyers and police officers) to pay attention when clues like these are given, and act before it's too late. In the Dorris case reported above, the estranged wife, Erdrich, could have done something to change things before the fact. Only she knows if she was the target.

---

[1] San Francisco *Chronicle*, April 15, 1997.

[2] In one of her books, she wrote: "If life's a joke, then suicide's a bad punch line." (Erdrich, L. "Religious Wars," *The Bingo Palace*, 1994.)

# FRIENDLY FIRE

Not just bitter rejection or unrequited love or public disgrace drives people to suicide. In a few instances, a work environment becomes toxic to someone who is sensitive enough to consider that environment the center of his or her life. Many more people than we care to admit are "married" to their work. This is the story of one poor man whose job meant more to him than anyone—least of all he— could admit.

The term "'friendly fire" entered common usage during the Vietnam War, to describe the phenomenon of a soldier being killed by a shot fired by his or her comrade-in-arms. Of course, this phenomenon has existed as long as there have been armies. On the battlefield, while most deaths are inflicted by the enemy, some occur by accident—as when a soldier's gun jams and explodes— but others simply result from being in the wrong place at the wrong time: "Sorry, old chap." The analogy with suicide is that some people are driven to kill themselves by their own colleagues, and this self-willed death is intended to punish a well-known tormentor once and for all.

As an example of an environment that fosters "friendly enemies," consider police work. In a televised interview, a cop, musing about the hazards of his profession, said that when he is driving down a street to respond to a disturbance call, he is less worried about being harmed by the person making the disturbance than (1) being sued or (2) being investigated by Internal Affairs.[1] Many police would echo this sentiment; if accurate, it means that "we have met the enemy and it is us." Add this to the fact that, each year, twice as many police kill themselves than are killed in the line of duty, and the conclusion is obvious: in some instances, cops kill cops.

As a case in point, consider the real-life tragedy of a Police

---

[1] This is a division within a police department, staffed by officers who are assigned to investigate crimes committed by other officers.

Captain in a large city, who killed himself at the age of 51, after 28 years on the force. I'll call this man Pat Kelly. In his city, many of the cops were Irish like himself, had come from the same Catholic boys' schools and attended the same Catholic university. Kelly moved smoothly through the ranks, impressed his superiors with his "command presence," and was given one leadership role after another until he was appointed Assistant Chief. He was well established in this position of authority when disaster struck. He was the officer in charge of the Traffic Division when a raging fire engulfed a high-rise apartment building. Every fire truck in the city was called out, but many motorists, in their panic and confusion, could not be moved out of the way to let the firemen through. Because of the delays in getting this fire under control, seventeen people trapped in the building died; it was believed that most of them could have been saved by swifter action. Years later, survivors of those who died were suing the city because the fire trucks arrived too late.

The fire department blamed the police, and the police department let Pat Kelly shoulder most of the blame. He was shown on local news, giving testimony to the City Council in which he defended the efforts of his fellow officers. Not long after, a new Chief of Police was appointed, and soon Kelly was demoted back to Captain and a job at a desk doing personnel work. Then, when there was an opening for the appointment of a Commander, a rank between Captain and Assistant Chief, Kelly did not get it. Shortly before he died, the city renovated its port facilities and created a new Assistant Chief position to direct police operations there. Kelly told several of his friends that he felt he should be considered for the post. What his chances were may never be known.

When Pat Kelly shot himself with his service revolver, his fellow officers pronounced themselves baffled. They said things like "There is nothing so serious that it would prompt him to do this," and "I can't figure this out," and "'It was a complete blind-side." In the eyes of some people, Kelly was a man who had done everything "right." His personal life was, to all appearances at least, above reproach, with a devoted wife and children. He came from the right ethnic background, went to the right schools, and had had no other career than law enforcement. He was destined for the role of cop and had given it his life—in more ways than one.

What can we learn from the sad story of Pat Kelly? Absent any evidence suggesting a different motive for him to take his own life, we can surmise that Kelly and his department had become adversaries to each-other. Perhaps a single disparaging comment from a colleague about Kelly's future with the department was the catalyst for his decision to kill himself. We know that something happened to lead him to this point of no return. The lesson of Pat Kelly's nightmare is this: jobs can kill, in the sense that a job consists in a web of relationships with fellow workers.

Imagine that a Martian had arrived before Pat Kelly died. The Martian, possessing an otherworldly ability to perceive what people feel, may have known that Kelly wanted to kill himself and sought to prevent it. He would interview Kelly's wife and children and other relatives, presumably without uncovering a vital clue. As the investigation continued, the Martian would learn about Kelly's problems on the job that surely began with the apartment house fire. It would soon become clear, to our insightful interplanetary visitor, that the answer might lie within Kelly's work environment. There might be found the moribund officer's designated target. What any conscientious Martian might have done about this potential suicide, once its cause had been found, is the subject of Chapters VIII and IX below.

# VII. THE CREATURE WHO COULD NOT DIE

Come away, O human child!
To the waters and the wild
With a faery, hand in hand,
For the world's more full of weeping
than you can understand.

—W.B. Yeats
"The Stolen Child"

I've never known a perfect person, but I've come across some perfect animals. What animals can teach us is what it means to live purely, with no wish to make of life more than it is. You come here to this planet, you take some breaths, and you continue on your way. In between, you see or hear some absolutely amazing fellow creatures and observe some astoundingly curious happenings. Animals have this connection with the world that we only dream about. If we watch a cat watching a bird, for example, we can imagine what it is like to wonder.

It may strike you as true to say that the most elusive question is "Why do we die?," but it doesn't elude an animal because no animal ever asks it. Naturally, an animal sees other animals die, and some are members of the immediate family, but we have no good reason to suppose that any animal expects the same fate. Without a concept of mortality, the animal is capable of concentrating on his or her life—improving its quality, staying alive—and sees no necessity to worry. Questions such as "How much longer do I have?" or "What will it be like when I am old?" do not trouble our animal friend. In short, no death, no brooding.

Animals come into the world in a state of innocence and will depart that way. No animal has committed a sin, and for that reason each is free of guilt. If no guilt, no need for redemption while alive, and no reason to fear punishment. It's hard for us to imagine what it would be like to be totally free of guilt for our actions. Only the saints among us have experienced such a state of grace, which for animals is a way of life. Unlike us, they do not see life as a "test" for some other form of existence. For them, life is.

In the story that follows, an animal goes against his true nature. As Fate would have it, he becomes too human.

In a place where you and I have never been, in a country we've never seen, there lived a Creature who could not die. He could fly like a bird and swim like a fish and run along the ground, but his favorite trick was hiding behind trees in his wood. One day, a ten-year-old boy named "Bucky, " who had been sent by his mother to find mushrooms, backed into the Creature who was behind a tree. You couldn't say who was the more startled, but after a while of staring at each-other, Bucky and the Creature began darting about as if they were playing a game, and soon they were laughing and taunting each-other by calling "over here" and then running off (I nearly forgot to tell you that this Creature could talk.).

The game of catch-me-if-you-can went on for quite a while, until Bucky realized that he'd have to go home and tell his mother that the rain had ruined the mushrooms; so, he said "Catch you later" and left the Creature behind a tree. He told his mother about this strange encounter with a talking animal—just like in the movies. Naturally, his mother feared for his safety and forbade him going to the wood alone. His father agreed that Bucky should be punished, not because there was any danger, but because he had become such a liar.

Even at ten, Bucky was feeling some of the rebellious urges of adolescence, and so he returned to the forbidden wood many times, each time finding his new friend behind the same tree. They became excellent friends and playmates, and sometimes the Creature would demonstrate how powerfully he could fly like a hawk high above the trees, and how he could navigate like a beaver the waters of a nearby lake. Their short visits together were filled with fun, and their trust in each-other grew naturally through many months.

One of the favorite games of these friends was to swim side-by-side in the lake. Bucky felt perfectly safe, certain that the Creature would save him if he became tired and couldn't make it to shore. They were swimming along one day when the Creature whispered to Bucky, "I'll tell you a secret: I cannot die." Bucky said nothing. He was shocked, bewildered, vaguely frightened by what he heard, but his first thought was that the Creature was capable of anything.

A few weeks went by, as Bucky pondered what the Creature had told him. The secret weighed on him a lot, and Bucky, being a normal boy, was aware that the one thing better than knowing a secret is telling it. Besides, he sensed that this Creature was not just an animal but some kind of Elemental Power. So, he confessed to his mother that he had gone to the wood alone to play with his friend, who had said "I cannot die." Bucky's mother, horrified, told the father, who erupted in rage (To this day, Bucky is not sure whether his father was angry at him for being disobedient, or angry at the Creature for being above dying.). Within hours, everyone in the pub knew about it, and soon the little town was buzzing with excitement. Here, at last, was the perfect scandal, perfect because not a living soul was to blame.

In time, Bucky's father became a town hero, because his boy had discovered 'the Creature who could not die, and the father had brought them the news. For his part, Bucky was mortified that this had become a *big deal*, and he apologized to the Creature, who accepted it with lightness of heart, saying "It's not your fault. I'm still your friend." They continued their joyful play times together, whenever Bucky could sneak out of school and run to the wood. Sometimes, he shared his lunch with the Creature, who enjoyed a change from his usual fare of berries and nuts. They had no foreboding of what Fate had in store for them.

With time, so many of the people of the town had expressed their outrage that there was a Creature who could not die, that vigilante groups formed to put an end to this mockery of God's will. Grown men armed themselves and set out to the wood to destroy this bird—or fish or mammal, whatever kind of monster it was. They soon found out that the Creature was as good as his word: not a shot from their rifles or shotguns found its mark. Though they stood in military ranks and fired fusillades in the general direction of the most recent Creature sighting, every bullet seemed to hit a tree or the side of a hill or a nearby farmhouse—the Creature was never there. Often, when they let loose a barrage of gunfire at ground level, the Creature would be sighted flying far above them. When they caught sight of him in the lake, their aim was equally erring, and when their ammunition ran out they shook their collective head and retreated home. As soon as he felt that the wood was safe again, Bucky ran in, and he and the Creature had some apple juice and went for a swim.

FLUMMOXED, read a headline in the local newspaper, reflecting the frustration of the townsfolk at not being able to curb this civic menace. And even though no one was sure what the menace was, exactly, the people joined in the belief that God's plan was that every form of life—even the giant redwood—should eventually wither and die. Only madmen or sorcerers would think of living forever. They turned to the elders of the town, pleading "How could this Creature escape our bullets? We must have hit him many times, but he showed no wounds and we found no blood. What are we doing wrong?" The elders were baffled, too, and could only suggest that the populace seek out the town Oracle for advice.

The Oracle, a woman who began her career in palmistry, was known to be difficult, but many people swore by her powers. They gathered in great numbers outside her cottage, calling for her to come out and help them solve their dilemma. The following is a complete text of the Oracle's remarks:

> Stand behind those barricades . . . stop crowding up here. You have a lot of nerve bringing this mess to me, whose thoughts are in the stars.

> You want my help. You'll get it, but you won't like it . . . come down from that tree.

> Yes, you have a problem. No, the Creature cannot die. Here are the notes from my trance: "No force without will make it cry. No human hand will make it die." That's when I woke up.

> The best advice I can give you about this Creature is to leave it alone. If you keep shooting at it, you'll kill each-other. Go home. Only pay me first. Thus hath the Oracle spoken.

A tall, ugly man named Atlas stepped forward and thrust a wad of bills into her hand. Everyone knew Atlas, who owned the town's only bowling alley and was an acknowledged bully, especially to his wife and children. People joked that Atlas would be the last to take the Oracle's advice, and in fact he soon became a leader in the group of diehards who vowed to carry on until the Creature could be caught, killed, and handed over to the taxidermist.

On a day when, unluckily, Bucky was at home in bed with measles, Atlas and his mates got a huge fishnet and trolled it across the lake when the Creature wasn't looking. Before he could cry out or swim out of danger, the Creature was captured and taken to the cellar of Atlas' house. There began a campaign of intimidation, terror, and physical torture that would have warmed the heart of Torquemada. These villains chained the Creature to a wall and tried to beat him with baseball bats, but to their consternation they landed not a single blow. A knife, wielded vehemently, would stop inches before it reached the Creature's chest, with no harm done and the wielder of the knife left to curse his luck. An electric charge, applied to the Creature's head, ran backward through the circuit, causing a blackout of the entire region. The townspeople, who had supported Atlas in his "experiments" until now, felt that he had gone too far when they lost their electricity, and took to calling him "Cluelas" or "Bowling Ball Head," or other nasty names. This made Atlas even more defiant and increased his desire to find one weakness in the Creature that would prove fatal. When his downtrodden wife asked "Why do you want to kill him?," Atlas answered "Because he's alive."

When Bucky recovered, he learned what was being done to his friend, who was doing it, and where. He decided to help him escape, and laid his plans carefully. He had to wait several weeks, but on the 30th of April, Walpurgisnacht, Bucky loaded his wagon with a huge barrel of beer, took it to Atlas' house, and shoved it through a window of the cellar, calling out to the Creature in his cage "Stay cool. I'll be back." Bucky knew that on that night the men would be carousing, that they couldn't resist the free beer and would soon be incapacitated by drink.

The plan worked so well that the two friends were able to tie one foot of each torturer to the foot of another, arranging them in a circle so that if one moved the other would fall over. It was in this state that the villains were found next morning. On the way back to the wood, Bucky told the Creature how much he had missed him and asked what the worst part had been. "I knew they couldn't hurt my body," replied the Creature, "but what they said to me hurt so much that I couldn't sleep. Because I didn't say a word to them, it made them even more furious. They made fun of my appearance, saying 'You're a cross between an antelope and a cantaloupe,' and they said cruel things like 'I'll bet your *parents* are dead.' They knew their words were sharper than their knives." Then the Creature began to cry softly, and Bucky realized that he had never before seen him show any emotions but enthusiasm or joy. Growing silent, they ate some muffins and split a can of soda, and then Bucky had to go home.

Atlas was mortified by the shame of letting the Creature escape. He gathered his forces and promised to find his prey and destroy it next time. He borrowed one of the police department's favorite toys, a robot on wheels with a camera, guided by remote control, that he sent into the wood for surveillance. This frightened Bucky because it could sneak up on them, and he had to restrict his visits to nighttime, when the robot's searchlights would announce its arrival. All the while, Bucky's mother knew that the boy was going to see his friend in the wood, but she pretended not to; true blue, she led her husband to believe that Bucky had discovered the public library.

When his robot could not find the Creature—or Bucky, for that matter—Atlas posted a sign at the entrance of the wood:

---

# ! VISITORS BEWARE !
## SOMETIME THIS MONTH, THIS WOOD WILL BE BURNT TO THE GROUND

## THE LAKE WILL BE DRAINED

## DO **NOT** ENTER HERE

---

Nearly everyone in the town was offended by this threat, but no one could find the courage to rise up against it. Some were reminded of the Inspector Javert, who hounded Jean Valjean in *Les Miserables*. Worse yet, they feared that this guy, Atlas, would become obsessed with *them*.

When Bucky saw the sign bearing Atlas' threat, he tore it up and told the Creature what he had seen. Bucky said, "You must want to kill him." "No," said the Creature, "I've never killed anything. In a way, I feel sorry for Atlas because he faces death every day and I don' t. In another way, I hate him as I hate any hurtful person. My revenge will be sweet. Creatures like me know how to get even." He told a funny story about how his ancestors plotted to get rid of the dinosaurs and blame it on an asteroid. Even though Bucky was reassured by the Creature's courage under fire, he had an intuition that something was wrong, and that his friend had come to some sort of crossroad. In the next few days, he noticed that the Creature would make excuses about not wanting to share lunch with him, and as time went on he saw less and less evidence that the Creature ate anything. Before his eyes, the Creature seemed to become both thinner and smaller, and there were times, when Bucky looked through the wood to find him, that the trees seemed to have gathered him up to give him shelter.

Afterward, Bucky realized that he had watched his friend starve himself to death. One day, he found the Creature's lifeless body in a sleeping position, hiding as always behind a tree. The boy's sorrow was profound, but he was brave enough to know that he would have to act quickly before Atlas found out. He went back to his house to fetch his wagon, and took the Creature to the wildest, most remote part of the wood. Digging a hole for the grave, he decided to bury the Creature in the wagon, because he didn't want his body to lie in that wet ground. There had been an envelope near the place where the Creature died, and Bucky knew that it contained a message for him, but he couldn't bring himself to read it now, stuffing it into an inner pocket. He hid the grave as best he could and went home, put the covers over his head, and cried and cried.

Bucky's mother sensed that her boy was grieving, but she was afraid to ask if something had happened to his friend. For his part, Atlas pressed on with his search; like Don Quixote pursuing windmills, he would roam through the wood, muttering to himself and shouting curses at the Creature who would not die. (Bucky couldn't help thinking that the torturer had become the tortured.) When Atlas reached the end of his tether and "snapped," he and his gang drained the lake and burned the wood to the ground. The townspeople came to see this destruction, and one of them discovered the Creature's grave. When they found the body cradled in Bucky's wagon, their thoughts switched back and forth between anger at Bucky and an odd sense of shame. Bucky's father was quick to point out to them that his son had done nothing wrong.

The people saw that the Creature had died from malnutrition, and they realized that he had committed suicide. They took up the animal's body and bore it away to a funeral home, where it would be given a proper casket and burial ground. They decided to have a memorial service although, later, many people asked themselves why. They felt a entire range of emotions, from bewilderment to a vague sense of dread. They tried to figure out what had happened since they first learned about the Creature, and what it meant for them. The more they explored their feelings, the more it occurred to them that they felt guilty for what had happened to this Creature. And since they knew that they had not caused his death, their guilt arose from what they had said about him, and what they had thought to themselves about him. It was then that they focused their attention on Atlas, who had not only thought the worst thoughts and said the worst things, but was the one who had driven the animal to killing itself. In this way, Atlas became the townspeople's scapegoat for the Creature's death, and before long he was being blamed for every aggravation from graffiti to bad weather.

Bucky didn't attend the memorial service because he knew he would cry, and when he was alone at home he opened the envelope, took out the Creature's note, and read:

When you find this, I'll be waiting for you behind a tree. I thought you might come to see me one more time. This is in case I miss you.

For a long time, you and I have been the best of friends. Believe me when I tell you that I was looking forward to being your friend for many years to come, watching you grow up and maybe, one day, you would have a son or daughter who could play with me here in the wood. As you can guess, I was planning to live a long time—forever—but it didn't work out. When I told you that I could not die, I believed it myself, but then I tried this method and it seems to be working.

Bucky, you have no reason to be sad today. The others will have their own sadness, and someday they will know why: they drove me from this Earth I love.

I wish you only happiness. But please don't look for me behind the trees in the wood. Don't search for me dancing in the sky. Don't wait for me at the lake in the mist of morning. You won't see me there—or anywhere. I'll be where you are. I'll be in you.

Moral: sometimes, only a child stands between you and suicide.

# VIII. THE TARGET

When times get rough
And friends just can't be found,

Like a Bridge Over Troubled Water
I will lay me down...

When darkness comes
And Pain is all around,
Like a Bridge Over Troubled Water
I will lay me down.

—Paul Simon
"Bridge Over Troubled Water"

When someone tells you about thinking of suicide, your life may change in ways that you never expected. Depending on the credence you give to the remark, you may have been handed an opportunity to save a life. Firefighters and police officers, paramedics and nurses and doctors may have a chance to do this often, but for them it is a job. For you, hearing a threat like this is a challenge to your humanity, and what you do will be out of the goodness of your heart. Think of it as equivalent to being chosen to serve on a jury in a death penalty case: the stakes are just as high, and your responsibility just as deep. Imagine that others have traveled this same road, because if people did not come forward to help suicidal persons, there would be many more successful attempts. You are in good company.

Knowing why people kill themselves, the reader will now be emboldened to try to save a life, if the occasion should arise. It's like the feeling that most people have after completing a CPR course: you may not remember exactly what to do a week later, but you are certain that if called upon you will do *something*. This part of the book is to guide you through the effort to keep someone alive who has threatened suicide—in short, a manual for Lifesavers.

# THREAT

Make no mistake about it, when you hear a threat of suicide from a friend or relative, it's better to take it more seriously than less. Most people who eventually killed themselves had talked about it with others before the act, often not straightforwardly but obliquely. After the death, survivors remember odd snippets of conversation with the message encoded in statements that, at the time, didn't make much sense. Some take the form of fatalistic comments such as:

"...if I'm not around."

"I'll never live to see that."

"Maybe I'll see you soon."

"You never know what might happen."

By themselves, statements like these might not be reflective of suicidal thinking, but if they strike you as having been more frequent lately, there may be a warning sign in them for you.

Some people reveal their intentions by gross behavioral changes, such as a sudden rigid streak. Perhaps the person will insist that the attorney finalize a divorce, or refuse to let a child off restriction, or demand that a debt be repaid at once. People say things like:

"You might as well sell this car."

"I am not having that cat in this house."

"I've got to finish this quilt [deck repair, family album, correspondence course]."

What is happening here is that the person is determined to set some things "at rest," especially those things that have recently been important to him or her, or to complete tasks that have often been postponed.

There is much to be learned about these subtle clues to suicidal intention, in the coping behavior of those who are terminally ill. They have been told that they have only a short time to live, and most begin immediately to put their houses in order. They want to make sure, above all, that their lives will "count" for something, which is part and parcel of wanting to be thought well- of when they are gone. They dwell a lot on what will be done with their worldly goods, and they ponder what their legacy will be in the minds of those who live on. The suicidal person, by contrast, has condemned himself or herself to an early exit from life, and only he or she knows how soon it will be. Similar planning for the person's posterity occurs, but the suicide takes pains to conceal it. The problem for the lifesaver is to cut through this deception with laser-like insight. If you have a sense that the friend or relative is acting like someone who has been diagnosed as being terminally ill, rely on your intuition and assume the worst possible outcome.

Don't be surprised if the person whom you suspect of being suicidal is suddenly tolerant of an enemy, or even speaks well of people whom he or she hates. The suicide is in the unique position of knowing that, by this self-chosen death, old scores will be settled and old debts repaid. He or she can afford to be magnanimous toward an intended victim today, knowing for sure that that person's judgment day is coming. This, by contrast, is a luxury that the terminally ill person does not share, because the latter believes that an enemy will be glad when he or she is gone. The suicide knows that it will be the worst day of the target's life.

Figure 3. summarizes some of the major observations that one might make of a person who is forming a suicidal plan.

**Figure 3.**

## DANGER SIGNS

If the clock strikes thirteen, you know that something is wrong. Here are thirteen behavioral signals that will confirm your suspicion that a friend or relative might be suicidal; the person:

1. is involved in a mutually destructive relationship, or cannot let go of a relationship from the past;
2. speaks in absolute terms about the other person, as in "She never did understand me" or "It's finished with him," or "I'll never escape from that woman";
3. expresses frustration with people in general, describing them in cynical terms such as "People don't change" or "You can't trust anyone."
4. is frequently nostalgic, reminiscing about significant events in his or her life, or returning to significant places as if to say goodbye;
5. starts giving people advice about what direction their lives should take, as though he or she wouldn't be around to advise them later on;
6. insists on concluding pending business matters, such as finalizing a sale or transferring titles or setting up a trust fund for a child; and, of course, makes a will when in perfect health;

7. begins to sort out short-term and long-term projects, keeping the ones that are "do-able" and discarding ones that might take a while to complete;

8. calls an old friend with whom he or she has lost touch, or visits a grandmother for the first time in years;

9. becomes inexplicably generous, giving away possessions to people, much to their surprise;

10. expresses newfound religious convictions, or heatedly denounces religion as "worthless";

11. becomes, if vain, super-vain; or, if normally unconcerned about appearance, downright slovenly;

12. seeks to persuade people that the crisis in his or her life has passed, and that there is no more need for worry;

13. suddenly becomes silent when asked what he or she is feeling, changing the subject by "shutting-out" or becoming distant.

The last of these is what the French call "la belle indifference," and is perhaps the most telling sign of all of what is about to happen. As a general rule, if you observe a majority of these changes in the person whom you are concerned about, consider it a cry for help. No harm will come from asking the simple question "Are you thinking of killing yourself?," phrased in any way comfortable to you.

## THE SEARCH

If you have a suspicion that some of the statements or aspects of the behavior of your friend or relative hint at suicide, you will want to be certain. Your first task is to find the most troubled among the person's relationships. You can do this by "surfing the network" of relationships that are most important to the person, including those that, like a recently lost love, remain powerful in memory. Start by asking who are the key people in this person's life. Then determine which relationship is most likely to have become damaged beyond repair. You are looking for at least one person who has become targeted for destruction by your friend or relative. Some may prefer to find out who this is by asking the direct question: "Whom do you hate?"

At this point, many very caring people may decide to distance themselves from the entire mess, and leave the lifesaving to someone else. There may be a series of crossroads along the way when the mind tells you to abandon this mission but your heart tells you to carry on. If the heart wins, you may have to press further on the subject of current hatreds, because there could be more than one. You want to know which antagonist is despised more than any other. A roundabout way to find this out would be to ask the threatening friend or relative "If you could kill one person you know and get away with it, who would that be?"

You may find, to your amazement, that the hated object is not a part of the person's family or social life, but someone at work, such as a vindictive boss or a conniving co-worker. But the suicidal person may not be able to tell you about wanting to kill anyone if the object of hatred is someone from his or her past, such as a dead parent or abusive uncle. In fact, it sounds ludicrous to hold a grudge against someone who wronged you many years ago, much less against someone who died since it happened. And yet people kill themselves because of unfinished business from the past, whose "ghosts" haunt their lives perpetually—as will be discussed in Chapter XI.

When you have identified the most toxic relationship in the suicidal person's life today, find out its current status. The two antagonists may be engaged in an open warfare of words, or may have turned their backs in an effort to ignore each other. A true sign that they have reached a dangerous phase is when one person refuses to speak to the other; this deliberate shutting-out often precedes the sullen withdrawal ("silence of the heart") in which a suicidal plan is conceived. The relationship becomes "sealed over" and the lack of communication fosters infection. As you survey this situation, it may occur to you that you are entering a battle zone where no one should tread. You may wish to call for assistance, but it's my sad duty to tell you that there is not much to be found.

## DON'T CALL A SHRINK

If the suicide threatener is in therapy, part of your task will be to make sure that the therapist knows what is going on. While a therapist has a duty to preserve his or her client's confidentiality, you have no such obligation to your friend or relative unless, of course, you have promised to keep the threat a secret. We'll take whatever help we can get, when it comes to saving a life. The difficulty may come when not even the person's shrink can intervene effectively.

If the person who threatened *is* in therapy, you may ask yourself how the situation was permitted to deteriorate to this point. If the person asks you or gives you permission to tell the therapist about the suicidal feelings, you may wonder why he or she didn't do it already. When the person has no therapist and if you believe that the threat might be carried out imminently, you have essentially three options; you can:

- take the person to the Emergency Room of a general hospital or the Intake desk of a mental hospital; or, failing that,

- talk him or her into finding a therapist or enrolling at an outpatient clinic; or, failing that,

- persuade the person to call a hotline when the impulse recurs.

Here's what will happen if you choose one of these options. The general hospital will send you at once to the nearest mental hospital. The mental hospital may take in the threatener, but he or she will very likely be back on the street before morning, having learned to tell the staff what it wants to hear—a promise not to "go through with it." A clinic will send the person to a psychiatrist, who will probably write a prescription for one of those anti-depressants mentioned above. A psychologist or marriage counselor will probably refer the case to a psychiatrist for the same reason: belief in the formula "no drug, no cure" for self-destructive thoughts.

The cause of this confusion rests with the background of most therapists, whose lack of training in the subject of suicide was referred to above. Suffice it to say that it's not a subject they relish, and there is no colleague in my acquaintance who advertises for self-destructive clients. The hotlines are no use, either: they are staffed by thoroughly conscientious people, nearly all of them volunteers, whose soothing, accepting voices can convince the caller that *someone* cares. The difficulty is that they ask the wrong questions, chiefly because they haven't a clue about what truly suicidal people think and feel. They are guided by mentors like Shneidman, who wrote that a potential suicide should be asked "How much do you hurt?" Questions like that, along with "Have you been depressed lately?" reveal to the person who is calling that no help can be expected from this source. Moreover, a majority of those who call hotlines are people who want to tell their troubles to someone and have no intention of committing suicide. When the radio talk shows have gone off the air, the hotline operator will always lend a sympathetic ear.

The person whom you are trying to save will not find comfort in any of the "helping professions," mainly because the taboo against suicide affects these practitioners in the same way that it influences the public. People find the subject distasteful and wish it would go away. The threatener will be stigmatized as a manipulating coward. The poorly-disguised anger that is represented by a threat is sensed by others and they are frightened by it. It causes them to think about the unthinkable. In short, what we *know* about suicide, deep inside, is the scary part.

Truth be told, there is no profession, agency, or institution in Western culture that is capable of preventing people from killing themselves, including major religions. Your suicidal friend or relative knows that "no power of Heaven or Earth" can make a difference. Even so, because you are aware of the taboo and what it causes people to feel, and because you understand these feelings and are not afraid of them, the buck will finally stop with you.

## THE THREATENER

When you find the source of the trouble in one of the threatener's relationships, the real task of saving a life begins. Your job is to heal the disabled relationship by changing one or both of these adversaries. People resist change, so your intervention may not be an easy one. By stepping in between a threatener and his or her target, you may feel like the referee in a sumo wrestling match, where the motto is "Don't get squished."

At some point, you will have to confront the threatener with your suspicions about him or her. You might as well be honest about it: "What you said has got me worried. I keep thinking that you could actually do it. I don't want that to happen. I don't want you to be dead. I'm going to do what I can to keep you alive." Tell the threatener (X):

> If you kill yourself, it will be because you hate someone.
> You wouldn't care if that person dropped dead today.
> I'll find out who that person is (Let's call the person Y.).
> If you killed yourself, everyone would know it was Y's fault.
> I plan to tell Y what you intend to do.

Having said these harsh, accusatory words and having yourself issued a threat, you will have to use the leverage of your friendship with the threatener, or the bonds of family membership, to see you beyond this point. Your aim, of course, is to mediate between

the two combatants, and to do that it will be necessary to persuade the threatener that something might be gained by media-
tion. As you well know, it will keep him or her alive, but he or she
might already have given up on the prospect of staying alive.

You may have noticed that there are no secrets in this approach to preventing suicide. There is no time for dancing around
the subject by asking questions such as "You're pretty desperate,
aren't you?" But while there is no need to mince words, the threatener is not being told that he or she is a villain or crazy in some
way. If you take care to let the person know that you don't consider him or her to be either mad or bad, it will go a long way
toward getting you the trust that you need for what lies ahead. Let
the person know you are aware that good people can have evil
thoughts. The rapport that you wish to re-establish after having
confronted the threatener as you have, will depend a lot on the
proof that you are not being judgmental, but only want to avert a
catastrophe.

## WARN THE TARGET

It's not a simple matter to say to someone, even someone whom
you know well, "You have an enemy who wants to destroy you."
But that, after all, is the message that must be conveyed. Tell the
target (Y) that:

1. X might commit suicide;

2. this is a serious matter;

3. something is wrong in your relationship with X;

4. X has developed an abiding hatred for you;

5. if X dies by suicide, he [she] will arrange it so that others
   blame you for the death;

6. X is trying to frame you for murder;

7. if you want to prevent this, there will have to be changes
   in your relationship with X.

By itself, warning a potential target is probably not enough, because in most cases he or she will not accept the role that the
threatener has assigned. In many instances, these two people will
have been at-odds for years before one makes a decision to end the
relationship in a tragedy for both. You may be called upon to
intervene quite forcefully in this entangled knot of misunderstand-
ing and animosity.

# THE BRIDGE

You have come to the point of confrontation between two antagonists who have a history of conflict and bad blood. You try to
get them together at some neutral site. Soon you might be in the
same room with a man and the lover who spurned him, or a wife
and the husband who betrayed her with another woman, or a
father who disowned his gay son and the son himself. You have
taken the role of physician-on-duty in this emergency room of
relationships. This is what becomes of people who can't get along
with each-other and turn their differences into obsession. They are
locked into a mortal struggle in which, one of them believes, dying is the only way to win.

If you bring these people together, take precautions for your
own safety. *You* aren't self- destructive, and you have no intention
of being wounded by the crossfire. Mediators and labor arbitrators
and hostage negotiators are very aware of the tendency of people to
turn against a Good Samaritan, because of needing a convenient
outlet for their feelings. One of the first rules of procedure for the
hostage negotiator is never to permit oneself to be taken hostage.
The lines must be drawn early and firmly with these two people
who are your guests: they are the ones who have a problem, and

this process is their chance to find a solution. Both must acknowl-edge that your only role in this is to help.

In the meeting, while you may be a sounding-board for one person and then the other, you are not a message-carrier between people who don't speak the same language. You refuse to "Tell the son-of-a-bitch that I think he's a piece of ___." If one person wants to vent that kind of anger to the other person, he or she must say it directly to the other. Naturally, rage has been trapped at the core of this relationship and must come out eventually, but it is far better expressed in words than in blows. Subconsciously, both people realize this, and if only they can stop being hateful toward each-other sufficiently to call each-other names, they will sense that they are closer to a truce than they have been for a long time. Let's face it, even if they beat each-other up in the parking lot on the way home, it's better than one of them "waking up dead." Here, I am doing my best to convey to you the suffocating tension that can exist between a potential suicide and an intended victim. The good news is that out of this cauldron of animosity can come a positive result.

For this confrontation to be successful, two critical events must occur: one person must apologize and one person must forgive. To put this into perspective, consider that the person who threatened suicide *does not want to die.* In fact, wanting to die is the least of motives for voluntary suicide. This person accepts death as the *quid pro quo* for the chance to carry out a larger plan. This person has long believed, with a growing passion, that the enemy who wronged him or her will never be sorry for what was done. For instance, the man whose father has not spoken to him for ten years is convinced, beyond all the efforts of others who try to tell him that he is wrong, that the father will never change and doesn't want to change. Even if his father would speak to him, he is cer-tain that the father would never apologize for what he has done. It is this certainty that has led the son to self-destructive thoughts, and must be proven false. As the mediator, you can help the rejected son to realize that this may be his last chance to get the apology that he needs to forget about suicide and stay alive.

The other partner in this contest of wills, the potential target, must decide whether or not to apologize. In the example, the obdurate father would say something like "I'm sorry I cut you out of my life. I apologize for all these years." The words are not important, just the feeling that the tone, the eyes, the body language conveys. In turn, this apology must be accepted by the threatener. And if the process goes as planned, acceptance of the apology will be followed by an offer of forgiveness. The prodigal son will say something like "Thank you for saying that. You hurt me more than I can ever tell you. But I forgive you." Again it is not the words that count, but the music of the way they are spoken. Forgiveness is the natural response to an apology, and the saving-grace of any conflict. As a human act, forgiving is without flaw. In the abstract, it is the basis of most religions, for which forgiveness of sins is necessary to receive the reward of eternal life.

Down here on earth, the two people whom you have brought together to reconcile their differences may do nothing of the kind, being incapable of either apologizing or forgiving even when a life is at stake. After all, they may have been fighting this duel for years before you came along. Remember that you are not their counselor or therapist, and do not need to be. What you have accomplished by the confrontation is to tell them that at least one other person knows what is going on between them. By now, they realize that their relationship is potentially lethal; no one remains naive when faced with killing or being killed. If you try to change this *relationship* and it doesn't work, the next step is to change the mind of the *threatener*; the chapter that follows will be your guide. As the saying goes, if the bridge falls in the river, use the good wood to make a boat.

# IX. ONE ON ONE

I get by with a
little help from
my friends.

—John Lennon and
Paul McCartney
"With a Little Help from
My Friends"

Confronting a potential suicide with the truth of what is about to happen is as perilous a task as taking a gun out of the hand of a potential murderer. It requires a steely eye and a steady hand, and if you succeed there may be no more result than creating a non-event. Even so, because removing a negative is a positive, you may decide to give yourself some credit as a suicide preventer. Your task is to intervene between a violent threat and lethal action. With a bit of luck, you will be able to save two lives with one heroic effort.

A simple formula for what you have set out to achieve is described by Figure 4.

For the events in this schema to occur as programmed, there can be no missing elements. For example, your involvement in the relationship between these two people begins when you become aware of the threat that one of them has made. You realize that your best strategy is to convince the potential target to offer some form of an apology to the threatener. If this apology is not accepted and does not evoke an offer of forgiveness, the sick relationship may get worse.

Figure 4.

SAVING LIVES

When you sense that the potential target is not prepared to cooperate, and that no apology will be forthcoming, you need an alternative plan to the one outlined in Figure 4. For this new plan, you will rely on the strength of *your* relationship with the suicidal person. Your commitment to keeping him or her alive doesn't stop at sundown, and may require a 24-hour vigil until the crisis is past (This is exactly what happens in a hospital or jail when the person is placed on "suicide watch."). Decisive action on your part may be necessary right away, and your approach may have to be blunt. Tell the threatener that you are going to give him or her three good reasons for not doing it, namely: it's futile; it's cruel; and, it will bring only disgrace.

## Futility

The suicide plan will fail. It will fail because everyone knows what you are trying to do, including your target. These people will not let happen what you want to happen. In short, the people whom you want to hurt will not be hurt. For example, one of these scenarios might follow your death:

1. Your wife will see your death as an opportunity to pursue her

relationship with her lover; what you thought would make her a slave to your memory, will set her free;

2. The partner who cheated you out of your share of the business will take everything, and you, the only witness who could condemn him, will be dead.

3. Even if you reveal, in your suicide note, that your father molested you when you were a little girl, no one will know what to believe; because no one saw what happened, you are the only witness to what he did to you; given the tendency of people to avoid "getting involved," you will be seen as a spiteful daughter, and your father's reputation will survive intact.

The point being made here, to the suicidal person, is that some sacrifices are not worth making. It will soon occur to this person that losing one's life is the ultimate empty sacrifice.

## Disgrace

Everything that you feel that you have accomplished in your life until now will be wasted. Your name will be mocked and your achievements denounced as worthless. People will say things like this:

> "He was a failure in life. When things got too tough for him, he took the easy way out; by killing himself, he proved what everyone had thought about him—he was a coward."

> "She was unable to appreciate what life had to offer her. She was never satisfied. In the end, she not only wasted her life but let everyone down who depended on her."

> "Because of what he did and the way he did it, our feelings toward him changed forever. He left too much bitterness behind."

"The jerk deserved to die. He did us a
favor by doing it himself."

"She only thought of herself."

People who say things like this after those close to them have killed themselves are adept at utilizing the defense mechanisms of denial ("no big deal")or rationalization ("we're better off"). Others are not so lucky and find themselves groping for answers to questions like "What have I done?" People like these are the true targets of suicide and, as we shall see in Chapter XI, they feel a numbing confusion that nothing will dispel. It is fair to say, to a threatener, that what he or she is thinking about doing is unspeakably cruel.

## *Cruelty*

The plan to kill yourself is stupid, because people whom you don't want to hurt will be hurt. Many people you know, who don't deserve to be punished, will be punished to some degree. Think of it this way: no one whom you truly love will survive intact when you are dead; that person will be changed in ways you cannot foresee. In short, person A will suffer for no reason except that you wanted to punish person B. Person A is an innocent bystander, who doesn't deserve your hatred.

For example, people will say:

"I know he couldn't stand it at work any more—with a boss
like that—but he should have thought of me and the kids."

"How could he do this to his family? Everyone knew he
hated that ex-wife of his, but couldn't he see how it would
hurt his mother?"

"No one can figure out what led my sister to do this. It's true
that her boyfriend dumped her, but all of us tried to help

her get over this—even our parents. Now we feel like failures."

There is nothing strange or unique about any of these reactions to
a suicidal death. They are the ordinary, predictable responses of
those who are left in the wake of tragedy, and who must accept,
however grudgingly, that they have a mess to deal with. These are
the "cries and whispers" of people who feel abandoned and, in
some cases, duped. We hear them in sound bites on the nightly
news or read them in newspaper accounts; they are no less poignant for their bitter tone. They reveal that the survivors of a suicide find it hard to grieve for someone so hateful. Even the suicidal
person may reach a critical stage when he or she realizes that one
or more reactions like these may follow upon the completed act. In
the worst case, a threatener who is confronted with the futility and
disgrace and cruelty of suicide will decide that even those outcomes
are worth it, and go ahead in spite of our efforts at deterrence.

Just as, in martial arts, one turns the opponent's strength into
a force against him, it may be necessary to tell the person exactly
what you think:

> "You are a 'player' who cynically manipulates people, a sa-
> dist who takes pleasure in punishing others, and a fool who,
> to achieve these ends, courts ridicule and shame. The worst
> part about you is that you are ungrateful, because you are
> willing to throw away the only gift you ever deserved—
> your life. You are a coward and a bully and a failure. Like the
> picture of Dorian Gray, you are monstrously ugly."

That is the extreme expression of the denunciation approach,
most useful when you sense that you need to get a threatener's
attention.

Another, often more persuasive approach, makes use of affirmation, in which the threatener's best qualities are praised. For
example:

"You have made a good life for yourself. You have kept your commitment to P, even though it hasn't been easy. You are loved and admired by Q, and R's faith in you has never wavered. In short, you have a lot going for you and people who care about you. Right now may be tough, but you've been through worse times than this. You made it then and you can make it now."[9]

If the person's thoughts are so obsessively vindictive that this line of argument has no impact, you may try to draw from his or her reserves of compassion as a last resort:

"Isn't there someone who needs you very much, who wouldn't know what to do—wouldn't make it—if you were gone? Are you aware that people need you? What about_____ or_____? What will they do if . . . Where will they go? Especially : who will look after him [her]?"

Everyone cares about someone. The task is to find out who that is and remind the threatener. Since life is unpredictable, you can raise the possibility that the person who is cared about may face some crisis and need help soon. If so, the helpee may have a chance to become a helper.

Every life is needed by someone. The message that a threatener must hear is: because your life is needed by at least one other person, it is needed by you. This reverses the logic by which a person chooses to "murder" someone else by self-murder. Beneath this irony lies a simple truth worth repeating: the person who threatens suicide does not *want* to die. Giving him or her an ex-

---

[9] When a young man, Hemingway wrote, in a letter, "...the real reason for not committing suicide is because you always know how swell life gets again after the hell is over." Some years later, he killed himself.

cuse—any excuse—for living may be enough to cancel that bargain with death. Not always does the potential target hold the key: it may be the *third person*.

## BITTER LEGACIES

Although it makes no logical sense, there are people who kill themselves for a different reason than to punish someone living, namely to settle a score with someone long dead. It is fair to call targets such as these "ghosts," and to prevent the suicide of a person who is haunted by them requires special skills. Naturally, one death scarcely deserves another, but the fact is that a person's death freezes relationships and seals them forever. Therefore, a relationship that was pathological cannot be changed, and the partner who remains may find nothing less than suicide to escape this prison.

When a person dies, he or she leaves a legacy of memories in the minds of those who knew him or her. These memories define a reputation, through the medium of the mental representations that people have of him or her and the values they assign to what the person was or what the person did. We say "After she died, I realized what she meant to me" or "I shall always remember the time when he . . . " Statements such as these describe the person whom we have lost but who remains vivid in our consciousness.

When we are not able to retaliate in real life for past hurts, we can attempt to influence the way people feel about a dead person. The hated father can be discredited in the eyes of those who knew him; the unfaithful spouse who caused so much humiliation when alive can be accused of a crime even worse than adultery—murder. This outcome can be achieved by killing oneself, but only if the target of suicide is clearly identified before, or by means of, the act. A striking example of how this is done was the case of the poetess Sylvia Plath, whose poem, "Daddy," "marks" her dead father; in the poem, she pours out her hatred for both the father and her faithless husband, his replacement, and in doing so explains her eventual suicide. In that act, she punished the memory of a dead man and poisoned the reputation of the one who lived on.[1]

When we find that thoughts of suicide are directed toward someone from the past, our first task is to find out who it was. Most people are not as self-revealing as poets are, but somewhere in the attic of the person's mind, hidden in the musk and cobwebs of memory, there may be a legacy of hatred that the person is determined to fulfill. A case in point would be that of a woman who was molested as a child by an uncle; the uncle was reported and accused, but not prosecuted for some reason; the incident was "swept under the rug" and became a family secret. From childhood to adulthood, this woman knew that the subject was taboo among family members, and, in turn, she swore her own husband to secrecy. When the uncle died, she felt free to tell others what had happened, but their indifference to what she had to tell them chilled her desire to resolve the trauma once and for all.

In time, this woman's efforts to cope with life's demands became compromised by various events that posed threats to her ego: her son ran away from home, she suspected her husband of having an affair, etc. Again and again, she returned in her thoughts to what her uncle had done to her. Because she had been given no opportunity to express her indignation and resentment when it happened, she felt cast in the role of perpetual victim: the wound had never healed. While she once thought that her uncle's death would set her free, it only emphasized that she was carrying the weight of unfinished business. She felt cursed. Leaving notes exonerating those who could not fairly be blamed, such as her husband and her son and her own parents, she killed herself in the name of the person who ruined her life. Only in this way, she thought, could the curse be removed. Ironically, her suicide accomplished in reality what the molester had accomplished only symbolically. The ghost of her uncle had triumphed from the grave.

If the woman in this story had spoken about her plan *before the*

[1] A detailed analysis of this famous suicide can be found in *The Anatomy of Suicide* (Everstine, 1998) pp.62-70.

*fact*, someone who wanted to help her stay alive could have tried to find out who the intended victim might be. If the search led nowhere, the possibility that she was trying to exorcize a ghost from her past would be worth considering. The question "Do you have a ghost?" is a legitimate one to ask any suicide threatener. If the answer had been "yes," and the woman had revealed that she was molested as a child, the focus of prevention would have been to persuade her that:

1. the past is past; this seems self-evident, but there are many people whose bad habit it is to live in the past (i.e., dwell on it, brood about it);
2. the past does not make rules, it only enlightens; this means that you can learn from what has happened to you, without being governed by it; in short, the only value of the past is to enrich the present;
3. this uncle, then or now, is not worthy of revenge; he did what he did not for sex or even to inflict pain, but instead for domination, control, power; to let it destroy you would be to confirm that power after all these years;
4. your uncle is dead, you are alive—you won.

This woman's experience in childhood may have stolen her innocence, but surviving it made her a stronger person. Her tragedy was that, because the experience was never worked-through, she was not aware that she was strong, and in fact thought the opposite of herself.

When trying to prevent the suicide of a person who is obsessed with a former relationship, as much as possible of that relationship must be exhumed, exposed to the light and air of the present day. "Did something bad happen to you when you were young?" is a standard question that many psychologists and psychiatrists ask in the course of getting to know a client. It's a way of opening a door to unfinished business, that often reveals information about legacies such as:

- traumatic events, including abuse of many kinds;
- rejection or abandonment by one or both parents;
- peer ridicule because of a physical handicap or deformity, or just being "different";
- something one did that injured or harmed another person, and could not be corrected or has never been forgiven.

Wounds to the psyche such as these can produce lasting scars, and even a perception of inferiority, on the part of the person who must live with them.

In many instances, people who have been emotionally wounded indulge in a type of wishful thinking that takes the form of a vow: e.g., "I'll show them," or "I'll pay him back someday," or the memorable "I'll never be hungry again" of Scarlett O'Hara. These pledges can become compulsions, and for some people they can be guiding principles that dominate their lives. Others take a different path, in which a history of cruel treatment or failure leads to the notion that one has been singled out for destruction by the gods. This was the situation of the woman who was molested by her uncle—forced to submit in the first place, and forced to keep silent until it was too late. The person believes that a curse has been placed on him or her forever, and wails "I'm a loser" or "I'm damaged goods" or "No one could love me." Rooted in a nightmarish past, the vow and the curse, fueled by anger, can be powerful engines of suicide.

Curses and vows, even though they can kill, are often life-enhancing sources of motivation. A poor child may take a solemn vow to lift his family out of poverty, and the person who dispels a curse can exult in a tremendous feeling of mastery and freedom. In helping someone to stay alive, positive forces such as these can be used to divert energy away from the suicidal plan. As in the example of the woman who was molested, she might have been told that the *only* way to defeat the curse would be to make a better life for herself than her attacker would ever have imagined. She could have been reminded that a vow to see her children through college would represent a victory over all her misfortune.

To some extent, these approaches to prevention are like swimming against the current, because each requires a reversal of a suicide threatener's mind set. If this person is seeking to punish a ghost from the past, a more direct strategy may be to create, for him or her, a *new past*. Therapists who find, in the course of treatment, that they have to help someone deal with unfinished business, often use this approach. They literally guide the person to a new interpretation of what happened many years ago. In this revision of history, a traumatic event becomes an unavoidable accident, having been abused reveals the weakness of the abuser, rejection becomes a fear of commitment on the part of the rejecting person, peer ridicule becomes peer stupidity, and a youthful error could only have offended those who lack compassion for human frailty. This is not brainwashing to convince someone that bad things didn't happen. Its magic lies in changing the *perception* of what happened, and this in turn alters the person's memory of the events themselves. By means of this variant of "reconstructive surgery," a therapist can gradually convert trauma into benign reminiscence.

As one who acts in the place of a therapist to save a life, your task is merely to change the way the threatener perceives a target who is no longer present. Repeating the theme "that was then; this is now," you can discredit the target in every possible way, drawing out the suicidal person's most rageful feelings. You can encourage a barrage of vilification of the hated object, providing a sounding-board for this cathartic process. You can lead the person to vent every conceivable negative feeling about the target, in this way purging the wound that has festered with the passing years. By demolishing this demon in the mind of a threatener, you will lead the person to the conclusion that he or she does not have to die to accomplish the same result. The power of a ghost lies in a person's belief that the ghost is powerful. In the absence of this belief, a ghost is no more than a shadow of its former self.

# X. DREAMCATCHER

Youth, which is forgiven
everything, forgives
itself nothing.

—George Bernard Shaw
"Man and Superman"

Adolescence is a misbegotten time of life that leaves scars on the psyche. Some do not survive. Through a series of ever more humiliating experiences, the young person is annealed for the fires to come. The physical challenges of puberty alone would be enough for this changeling to deal with, but the state of confusion that they engender is, in many instances, stupefying. Small wonder, given this degree of perplexity, that the teenager drifts into a fantasy life in which, on some terms, happenings make sense. Small wonder, indeed, that most cases of schizophrenia begin during adolescence, and that the per capita rate of adolescent suicides in America rises steadily, year by year.

What the young person cannot see, much less acknowledge, is that childhood is dying. He or she knows that something is wrong, but hasn't a clue about what. Adults are perceived as part of the problem, so why take advice from them? The adolescent is more and more drawn into his or her peer group, where the blind are eager to help the blind. To them, only change is real. It happens daily, with relentless force. They worship it: if they live in a democracy, a dictatorship would be preferable; if four earrings are boring, wear five.

Left to the mercy of peers, a teenager may be more vulnerable than in the world of adults that he or she has left behind. In *Lord of the Flies*, by William Golding, young boys are stranded on a deserted island and must fend for themselves. (The title is a translation from "Beelzebub," a Greek word for the Devil.) This story, a fable about man's inhumanity to man, tells of the boys' savage cruelty to each-other. The fable gains strength from an awareness that every one of us shares, but don't like to dwell upon: young people have a mean streak that, unless checked, can lead them to primitive acts of violence. Unlike animals, we do not do this out of necessity.

In the story that follows, a teenager becomes the pawn in a deadly game, invented by his parents, over which he has no control, and for which he has no coping skills. As luck would have it, this Hansel finds a Gretel, who helps him to escape from his Forest of Ilsenstein.

When Tristan was fourteen years old, his parents announced their plans for divorce. Tristan was naturally devastated. An only child, he was well aware that his mother and father had their differences, but he never expected that they would, in his words, "give up" on their marriage. When he thought about it, it struck Tristan that he was one-third of a family of which two-thirds were committing suicide. He felt lost, betrayed, cheated, cast aside, unwanted, helpless, and, somehow, furious. When he thought about it more deeply, he realized that neither his father nor mother was to blame, and least of all should he blame himself. It wasn't his fault. He had just been a dutiful son whose family had chosen to self-destruct. In his heart, he was certain that this nightmare would end some day, and that his parents would eventually come to their senses and get back together.

Apart from his naivete, Tristan was an exceptional adolescent. Tall for his age, he was the only Freshman on the high school football team, and a leader among his peers; as one teacher put it, he was seen by the other kids as "calmly confident." He appeared to have learned well the teachings of his parents and to have "the right values," including a forgiving nature.

As the struggle between his parents worsened, Tristan found it harder and harder to keep neutral in the midst of conflict. He "took sides" in their quarrel, but one day he would be on the side of one parent, and on the other side a day later. At first, this role merely confused him, but as time passed he felt more and more guilty because, it seemed, he could not help either parent; they got no closer to resolving their differences, and seemed determined to establish who would be the "winner" and who would "lose."

Suddenly, Tristan's father announced that he was moving to a city hundreds of miles away; Tristan could visit during summers and at important holidays. After his feelings of abandonment had subsided, with the passing of several months, Tristan began to adjust to this unusual situation. Indeed, he missed his father, but now he could be more protective of his mother—who, he had long suspected, was the more emotionally vulnerable of the two. Trying to help, he relayed messages from his mother's attorney and screened her calls so that his father would not talk to her when her defenses were down. The divorce became final, and Tristan felt himself ready for the new chapter in his life, as "survivor" of a broken home.

About a month later, the school held an "Open House" and Tristan's mother was persuaded, after trying to excuse herself, to attend with Tristan. There were some awkward moments because people knew about the divorce but did not know how Tristan or his mother felt about it. The next day, Tristan's teacher asked him to stay after school and said: "A student, a girl, came up to me last night and asked me a strange question. She asked me if your mother is pregnant. When I looked closely at your mother, I realized that she is. Believe me, I know the signs." Dumbfounded, Tristan blushed, stammered, and just managed to flee the situation before making a fool of himself.

By the time Tristan got home, he was crying, shaking with embarrassment, and filled with an amorphous rage. He confronted his mother, who declared that she was, in fact, pregnant. When

Tristan demanded to know who the father was, she fell silent. When he insisted, she said that she had promised not to tell anyone— not even him. Tristan ran to his room and disintegrated into alternating waves of sobbing and cursing. It was, he told himself, the worst day of his life.

But the worst was yet to come. First, his mother, grudgingly answering Tristan's frenzied questions, said no, she would not consider having an abortion; further, she had been told that the child in her womb was a boy. When the teacher called her to express concerns about Tristan, his mother admitted being pregnant and said that she had realized she could not conceal it much longer; in fact, that had been her reason for attending the Open House. Tristan would get used to the idea because he is a wonderful boy who has "everything going for him."

It wasn't long before the school was buzzing with talk about Tristan and his "knocked-up mother." Rumors flew as fast as the time when the kids discovered that two teachers were having an affair. Graffiti appeared in the boys' room and notes were slipped into Tristan's locker. Comments about the scandal became increasingly crude and malevolent. There were even threats of violence against the baby, Tristan's mother, and Tristan himself, proving that there is a little Nazi lurking in every adolescent. This climate of righteous indignation spread to kids in every grade and finally became an issue for the teachers, who met in a group to "assess" the situation. They considered asking Tristan to stay home from school for awhile until things "cooled off," but changed their minds when they realized that it might make matters worse. They summoned Tristan's mother, who was steadfast in her refusal to name the father, or even to use her opposition, on principle, to abortion as an excuse.

Tristan, who had known nothing but popularity and success, became a pariah among his classmates. No one wanted to be seen with him, let alone sit at his table in the cafeteria. The football coach took Tristan aside and said that he might hold him out of Spring practice this year, if "this business" might affect *team mo-*

*rale.* This last was the source of nightmares for Tristan, in which he would see the frowning face of his coach and conjure elaborate scripts of what his teammates were saying about him. To avoid dreams like this, he stayed up late playing video games. He lost weight and began to show dark circles around his eyes.

One day, a girl whom he hardly knew, Naomi, came up to him after school and asked if Tristan would walk her to her car. She was seventeen—a Senior—and very lovely, and Tristan felt himself blushing and dry of mouth, but, always the little gentleman, he walked silently along with her. Naomi did the talking: she said that she knew what was going on, because she had heard the rumors, and she hated it. She had seen the look on his face grow sadder for weeks now, and she was worried about him. At home, she had made something for him that might help.

Mystified, Tristan followed Naomi to her car, where she reached in and took out a hoop, the size of a pie-plate, that appeared to hold different-colored strands of string woven in a web-like pattern, with a small hole in the center. Handing it to Tristan, she said: "It's a dreamcatcher." "What's it for?," asked Tristan. "It's for you," she said, "to catch your dreams." "Thank you" was all Tristan could say while, holding the dreamcatcher as if it might break, he retreated from Naomi's car. "I've got to get home," he ventured, but Naomi shot back "Meet me tomorrow at lunchtime in the cafeteria and I'll tell you what the dreamcatcher means."

The next day, Naomi led the way to a table where they could be alone, and after they exchanged jokes about how bad the soup was, Naomi asked "What did you do with it?" "I gave it to my mother," Tristan replied. Naomi said "That's not what you're supposed to do. You hang it in the window of your bedroom. Get it back and look closely at it. What happens is that when you dream, dreams escape your body, going outward in all directions; the tiny hole in the middle of the web lets good dreams out into the world where they become reality. The bad dreams are too big and get trapped in the web; then the morning sunshine causes them to dissolve and disappear, and they never become real. That's an American Indian story."

"Cool" was all Tristan could say to this. He wasn't very good at expressing gratitude, but his heart was warmed by this person who seemed to be the only one who cared if he lived or died. If he was falling in love with this guardian angel, it was rendering him speechless. Later that day, daydreaming in class, Tristan realized that her gift had somehow deepened his humiliation, because, if a total stranger had seen how shaky he was these days, his close friends must surely be feeling sorry for him now. Tristan' s apprehension rose daily as the time for his mother to have her baby drew near. And just when he had begun to accept the notion that he was going to have a brother—even this brother—the school newspaper came out with a front-page article under the banner headline IMMACULATE DECEPTION. The article began: "The mother of one of our fellow students, who shall remain nameless . . . " It went on to set forth, in the tones of scandal, a chronology of events in the story of " . . . a well-known student whose identity will be protected in these pages." It posed a series of caustic questions about the prospect of the student's mother having a baby out of wedlock: was the father someone prominent in the community?; whose surname would the child be given?; how would "our anonymous classmate" feel about the birth of a BASTARD BROTHER?

The article continued with references to "virgin birth" and other vicious slurs on the wayward mother who had caused this crisis. There was speculation that the "hapless teenager" might even himself have gotten his mother pregnant. Rising to the height of his sarcasm, the writer speculated that, if the baby were a son, this "formerly popular person" would then be both its father and half-brother; indeed if the child grew up and had children of his own, the "onetime football player" would be their uncle and grandfather at the same time. Another article, enclosed in a box beside the main story, was an invitation to students to sign up for a field trip to the local cemetery, where they would visit "The Tomb of the Unknown Father," with a person identified only as "T" as their guide.

After reading this and stuffing the paper into his backpack so that his mother wouldn't see it, Tristan selected a strong rope from the garage of his house, put it in the backpack, and returned to the school. He sat in the Library until it closed and then waited on the roof until it was dark. He let himself in through a window and went directly to the cafeteria, where he turned on every light he could find. He stood on a dining table, made the rope into a noose for his neck, and tied an end of the rope securely to a light fixture. He shoved the table away from his feet, felt himself beginning to choke, and then fell heavily to the floor when the light fixture broke. Blackout.

He awakened in a hospital bed in a haze of dull pain. They told him that his leg was broken; he was lucky to be alive, because his head had struck the corner of the table when he fell; he had suffered a slight concussion and was found a short time later by the janitor. They told him that his mother was outside the room, and when he called out "Mom," she came rushing in. Her consternation and shock were evident on her face. She stood by the bed in utter frustration, reaching out but unable to embrace him because his leg was suspended in traction; she settled for kissing his hand. "My poor boy. I'm so sorry. I want to hold you . . . Why? What made you do it? Was it because of me? Was it because of this?"— her hand touched her stomach. Tristan burst into tears. "Mom, no—I love you . . . I tried to kill myself because . . . because— look in my backpack."

When she looked into the pack, she found a flashlight, a yearbook picture of Naomi, and the fateful newspaper. She could scarcely believe her eyes at what she was reading, turning several shades of purple as she paced around the room, holding the paper away from her face one moment and staring at it the next. "I'm sorry, Mom," said Tristan, "I didn't know." "Of course, you couldn't know," said his mother. "This is outrageous . . . Tristan, please forgive me. I'll find a lawyer. Don't tell your father, please. I have to go because they said he's coming here now. I'll be back tonight. My sweet boy, goodbye." She kissed him on the hand again and was gone.

In a short while, Tristan's father appeared. He was subdued, as he always was when frightened, and father and son exchanged only a few words (Tristan had hidden the newspaper under his pillow.). When asked why he had done it, Tristan mumbled something about kids at school giving him a hard time. The father seemed to accept this, asked him not to do anything like this again, and left. Later, his mother returned and sat at his bedside for a long while. She vowed to sue the school district, the Principal, and the parents of the children who wrote the articles. "Whatever it takes," she was saying when her son fell asleep. The hospital announced that it would be keeping Tristan for several days for "observation, " and explained to the mother that they had been unable to convince Tristan not to try suicide again.

The next day, Naomi came to see him, and he felt joyful but terrified that he might say something wrong. When Naomi asked some gentle questions about his injuries but nothing about why he had done it, he began to feel safe and would have told her anything. At length, she asked whether or not he was thinking of doing it again. Tristan replied that, last night, he had had a horrible dream: something came to him—"like an alien"—and told him that he had brought disgrace to the family; so, he must keep on trying to die to clear the family's name; if he was dead, people would take pity on his father and mother and maybe they would get back together again; with him out of the way, they wouldn't have anything to fight about. Sure, he'd do it again—the right way this time. The people who wrote that stuff about him would know what they had done; maybe the guy who wrote that article would kill himself, too. "That's all I can do for my dad and mom."

Naomi listened thoughtfully and said "I'm worried about the nightmare you had. Where is that dreamcatcher?" "Oh, she put that in the attic. 'What good is this?,' she said." Smiling, Naomi

softly wished him well, said that she would be back, and took her
leave as mysteriously as she had come. He could have sworn that
she was wearing moccasins, so silently did Naomi walk in and out
of his life. That evening, he awakened from a nap to see her standing beside the bed, holding the dreamcatcher. "I got this from
your mother, " she said. "I'll put it here, on this window, and
when you go home I want you to put it on the window in your
room. Is that clear?"

When they wheeled him out to the car a few days later, Tristan
was holding the dreamcatcher in his lap like a football trophy. The
nurses warned his mother that he had steadfastly refused to promise that he wouldn't commit suicide; they were worried that another attempt would surely follow. For her part, the mother was
having complications in her pregnancy and realized that she would
have to hospitalize herself soon, so that she wouldn't lose the baby.
She made an arrangement with her ex-husband to come "home"
so that someone would be there to watch over their son. Reluc-
tantly, the father complied and the mother left for the hospital.
Tristan, in a cast, stared out the window for long periods; in this
window was the dreamcatcher.

The night when his father arrived, the two of them had a
conversation, over dinner, for the first time in recent memory. Between long pauses and an occasional tear, they said:

"I thought you wanted to kill yourself because I left . . . because of what I did to you and your mother."

"Dad, I love you."

"What I mean is, I thought you hated me, but then she showed
me what that newspaper said . . . I guess you read it first."

"That's right. I didn't want anyone to hurt her again. That's
when I got the rope out of the garage."

After a heavy silence, Tristan asked "Dad, do you know who
the father of mom's baby is?"

"I know but I can't tell you," said the father.

"Do you mean you won' t tell me?"

"That's about it." Another silence was broken by the father, now sobbing uncontrollably: "You're not going to do it again, are you?" Tristan replied "I won't tell you," and the conversation abruptly ended.

As they waited for the baby to arrive, Tristan and his father rattled around their house like most enforced bachelors, bumping into each-other and avoiding each-other by turns. Tristan looked more lost with each passing day, even though he grew more nimble each day in walking with the cast on. The father watched in dread as his son became more and more somber and sullen, but he realized that there was nothing he could do to lift his son's gloom.

Naomi came over one day and brightened the room with her smiling presence. She saw the dreamcatcher in Tristan's room and asked him if his sleep had improved. "Sure, I sleep soundly. But lately I've been sleeping ten or twelve hours or all day. It's becoming a problem to stay awake. Anyway, no nightmares." When she asked when they could expect him back at school, Tristan said nothing but began to rock in his chair, rubbing his hands along his thighs in a ritualistic way. Naomi thought that he was not even conscious about what he was doing or how this compulsive behavior would be perceived by others. She reflected that Tristan could not possibly return to the school—he was trapped by pride and shame. She felt a chilling fear for this boy, who must certainly be planning to make it a successful suicide next time. She felt helpless, but the least she could do would be to warn the father that the danger of losing his son had reached a critical point.

As if to prove that the forces of life are stronger than the forces of death, Tristan's mother had her baby, a healthy boy. That was the first miracle. The second was that Tristan's father was present when she delivered the child, and promptly announced that he was the father. The third was that the mother acknowledged that, in fact, he *was* the true father; not only that, she would accept his offer of reconciliation. Armed with this news, Tristan sawed off his cast and enlisted Naomi to drive him to school, where they badgered the editor of the student paper to print a new story with the headline BASTARD NO MORE. The story that followed gave the paper a chance to say it was sorry for maligning "a fellow student who shall remain nameless," and had been wrong to cast aspersions on the family of this "popular sports hero." In closing, the editor sought to dignify the entire affair by writing: "Remember the words of Shakespeare:

> "If we shadows have offended,
> Think but this and all is mended,
> That you have but slumber'd here
> While these visions did appear.
> And this weak and idle theme,
> No more yielding but a dream . . . "
> ("A Midsummer Night's Dream")

Despite their differences, Tristan's parents did their best to explain to him what they had done. They had made a pact in which they would conceive a child before separation. The mother had wanted more children for many years; the father wanted to avoid the extra child support. If she would not reveal that he was the father, she could have her child. For them, it was a perfect arrangement, but in the emotion of the moment they failed to think it through. Tristan accepted their explanation with the teenager's ultimate put-down: "That's dumb."

Even though there was a difference in their ages, Tristan and Naomi grew up and married, having known from that first day that they were soulmates. They opened a store called "Midsummer Night" and sold dreamcatchers and all manner of mystical and fanciful inducements to peaceful sleep. Above the door was a slogan they had found in "The Tempest": "We are the stuff that dreams are made on." Their life together was unmarked by events like the one that had brought them together in high school, but they were especially sensitive to the fragility of their teenage children, and how vulnerable they were to the judgments of their peers. Moral: only by accident are many people still alive.

# XI. NEXT OF KIN

A suicide kills two
people . . . that's
what it's for.

—Arthur Miller
"After the Fall"

At some point along the way to saving a life, you may ask yourself
how you began on this path, how you got into this situation, what
caused you to accept this role. If you wrestle with self-doubts such
as these, remember that you are not only trying to keep a suicide
threatener alive, you are trying to shield a potential target from
harm. This other person is (or these other persons are) in psychological danger from the moment when the suicide plan is formed.
You have an opportunity to protect someone who has no idea what
lies in store.

What lies in store is well-documented in research on the survivors of suicide, people who have found out—the hard way—what
could happen to them at the hands of someone close to them.
That impact will be described in this chapter, not because it is
likely that you will be asked to heal the damage done to a survivor,
but to show in graphic detail what the suicidal person has in mind.
What suicide does *to* others is at the core of the suicidal motive. By
seeing that motive for what it is, you have a better chance to defuse
it.

The process of grieving is not the same when a person has died
by suicide, as it is when death was by natural causes—or even by
homicide or accident. The difference is that, by contrast with those

other deaths, suicide is the person's *own fault*. Grief over a suicidal death is qualitatively different from other kinds of profound loss (e.g., death of a child by pneumonia, a spouse killed in an accident, a youth being placed in a foster home because his parents were sent to jail). If you have had the temerity to visit the home of people who have lost a family member to suicide, you will have sensed their perplexity and fear. They are trying to figure out what has happened to them, searching their thoughts to decide whether or not a message was being sent by the dead person. If so, what was the message, and for whom was it meant? In practical terms, many survivors of a suicide will not find answers to these questions. Even so, the true target will know it and, in time, realize that his or her life will never be the same again.

To illustrate this dilemma on the part of suicide survivors, real-life examples are supplied by a research study that had an unexpected result. When the psychologist Marv Miller was working on his dissertation on the suicides of men sixty years or older, he encountered a significant number of refusals when he sent a questionnaire to a sample of the widows of these men. The stated purpose of collecting this information was to help prevent more suicides; but, not only did some widows refuse, they wrote indignant comments on the questionnaires and sent them back. Here are some examples:

1. "I choose not to. I'm trying my best to forget and I don't need to be reminded. I had a stroke shortly afterwards from shock."

2. "I'm trying very hard to overcome this horrible tragity [sic]. Please do not disturbe [sic] any farther."

3. "No, I do not won't [sic] to talk now or ever about this do not write me any more."

Some replies were more tersely adamant; others were written in huge letters across the questionnaire, heavily underlined, or written in red ink. The report of Miller's study concluded:

> "Many survivors of suicide . . . will not cooperate at all with researchers . . . In fact, they may seize the opportunity to vent their anger and frustration on the researcher as a desperate means of fighting the stigmatization so often faced by those [whose] close friends or loved ones have committed suicide."[1]

This shows how the rage that propelled the suicide is transferred to those left behind. Because the widows could not retaliate against the source of their anger, they projected it toward the researcher. The sad part is that these widows were probably unaware of what they were feeling or how they were expressing it. Very likely, they experienced a sense of having been accused of a nameless crime. As in a story by Kafka, they are prisoners in a cell without walls.

In his classic book, *After Suicide*, Samuel Wallace reported the results of his study of twelve other widows of suicide.[2] By means of face-to-face interviews, Wallace succeeded in persuading these women to give full accounts of their feelings since losing their husbands, as well as intimate details of their lives before the event. Wallace was able to tape-record some of the interviews, and this is an excerpt from one of them:

> " . . . when they did tell me, it was almost like unbelievable, like it was happening to somebody else, but really didn't happen to him, you know. It was just like I—like it was happening to some other family, but [laughs] not really happening to—and then when I DID realize that he had done it, it was just a HORRIBLE thing that was—you

[1] Miller, M. "The Numerous Ways of Saying 'No' to a Researcher of Suicide," *Psychology*, vol. 17, number 4, Winter 1980, pp. 37-39.
[2] Wallace, S.E. *After Suicide*. New York: John Wiley & Sons, 1973.

know, the feeling of it would just start at my toes and it would just work, you know, right up through my body, and I realized that I couldn't stand it, to think about him doing this.

" . . . the thought of . . . when, oh, I remember one time I was driving to work and just out of the clear blue sky, this just OVERWHELMING thing, you know, it just swept over me—what HE HAD DONE, and I, I just thought, OH, I'm going to go MAD.

"And I remember saying over and over, 'Oh my God, it's all my fault; it's all my fault.' I just kept saying this over and over again . . . " (p. 104).

In summarizing what he had learned from lamentations such as these, Wallace wrote: "The suicide of a conjugant is a life-threatening action, and it produces the most intense grief of any type of death. Some researchers call it 'complicated' and others term it 'acute' grief, but by any name its intensity is searing" (p. 229).

Generalizing from the results of his study, Wallace concluded: "Coping with suicide is coping with death, and although death always takes its toll, suicide extracts even a higher price, threatening the very lives of the living. When the suicide was your spouse, an already intense experience is further intensified . . . In life as in death, the suicide and the [spouse] left behind are inexorably drawn together. What life had joined not even death could put asunder" (p.3). This theme of the living dead permeates the stories of these twelve widows, and it epitomizes the plight of the target of suicide. It would be naive not to form the impression that the suicidal person knew full well what the result would be. If you are in the position of trying to keep a threatener alive, keep this in mind: this person is "mad enough to kill."

A psychiatrist named Sue Chance wrote a book, *Stronger than Death*, about the death of her son by suicide.[1] The son, Jim, was 25 when he died, and because the mother had not been particularly close to him in the months preceding the event, her narrative of what led up to it is largely second-hand; most of the book describes her own feelings at the time and for several years afterward. Here is Dr. Chance's account of what happened on the fateful day:

> "He was always considerate–even in the way he blew out his brains.
> "He started his note, 'I love you all,' and made it clear that nobody was to blame but him.
> "He left the house after everyone was asleep, drove to a park just outside town, parked his pickup in a conspicuous place, sat on the riverbank and drank a six-pack as fast as he could, then stretched out full length, put the .38 Derringer to his left temple, and pulled the trigger.
> "The blast that ended his life started a shitstorm for his family" (p. 10).

The hostile undercurrent in this statement is hard to ignore. If Jim were a spiteful person, he came by it honestly.

The book goes on to reveal the mother's feelings more candidly. She quotes a poem that she wrote for Jim, which was read aloud by a minister at the funeral; one verse goes:

> "You are gone
> And you are with me
> I carried and I carry
>     you inside me
> Even though you aborted
>     my future

---

[1] Chance, S. *Stronger than Death*. New York: W. W. Norton, 1992.

with your precious
beloved self"

(p.28).

Here, the implication is that, because she did not abort Jim, it permitted him to "abort" her life. After the funeral, Chance began to address the question of assigning blame for the devastation she was feeling, and the first person to be singled out as a possible culprit was the venerable St. Augustine. She noted that, while the Bible does not explicitly prohibit suicide,[1] it was Augustine who condemned it as a sin. As a result of the doctrine handed down by this Bishop of the Fourth Century, her son would be sent to Hell and his death thus robbed of any dignity.

The next object of the doctor's anger was her own father, Jim's grandfather. This man and Jim's grandmother had raised him since he was eleven. When Chance found out that her father had known about Jim's suicidal feelings for at least a year before he died, she became outraged: "I felt like killing my father." What most upset her was that " . . . he was, in essence, denying his heavy contributions to Jim's suicide" (p. 29).

As time went by, Chance found another villain than her father—Jim himself: " . . . I got very angry at Jim. I was in a towering rage the whole third year of my bereavement" (p. 146). In her book, she catalogues his deficiencies:

"To survive the suicide of someone you love is to understand irrevocably that, in nearly every case, it is an act of
cowardice . . . That, far more than my inevitable failures as a
parent, is what I'm ashamed of. The fact that my son was a
coward" (p. 52).

Worse yet, she attributes to Jim more than mere weakness. He

---

[1] Remember the Zero Commandment (Chapter IV), which was never written down because it seemed so obvious.

*intended* to harm those whom he left behind: "Jim was a traitor to me. He was a traitor to everyone who loved him" (p.51).

After her period of "towering rage" exhausted itself, Chance entered a philosophical phase: "Here's a bit of news for you," she writes, "Suicide occurs in healthy families" (p. 108). This is a way of saying that having a suicidal son is some trick of Fate, for which no one bears responsibility. The paradox in this case is that Jim did not come from a healthy family. Chance had been married at the age of fifteen, gave birth to Jim when she was seventeen, divorced his father when she was nineteen, and got married again the same year. Jim was adopted by his step-father, but the marriage ended when Jim was eleven, and he went to live with his grandparents. His mother, who was determined to prepare herself for a career, began college in a year when she was also serving as Jim's Cub Scout den mother; when he began high school, she went off to medical school. Here was a mother who abdicated her role as a mother, maybe because she had never truly embraced it. Perhaps she had, as suggested by her poem, given some thought to having an abortion when she first learned that she was pregnant with Jim. But even if Jim did not feel like an orphan, even after being abandoned both by his father and his step-father, he must have felt some confusion at having a mother who was " . . . always being mistaken for his older sister" (p. 31).

The sad story of Dr. Chance and her lost son would serve as a cautionary tale if it were not so distasteful. We can clearly see the mother's moral bankruptcy, in her pathetic attempt at saving face by writing a book. The idea of doing so carries its own elitist, condescending tone. Not many people have the luxury of writing a book to purge themselves of their guilt. The ironic part is that, if you have to write a book, you don't "get it." What you don't get is that the game is already over—checkmate.

If Dr. Chance's explanation of the death of her son qualifies her as the Eternal Target, others fit this archetype as well. One such is Ted Hughes, husband of Sylvia Plath, whose suicide was mentioned in Chapter IX. When Sylvia, an American, married the

Englishman Hughes, also a poet, they settled in Britain, had two children, and became a kind of First Family of English Letters. The tragedy began when Hughes left her and moved in with another woman. Some time later, Sylvia, sparing the children, stuck her head in the oven and turned on the gas.

While it was never clear whether the primary target of her suicide was Hughes or the "ghost" of Sylvia's father, there is evidence that Hughes thinks he was "it." For more than thirty years after her death, he wrote a series of poems to her and about her, finally publishing it under the title *Birthday Letters*. During this time, he gained fame in his own right, rising to the honorary position of Poet Laureate of England. Why, then, would he have labored so mightily in Sylvia's name, if it were not to expiate his feelings of guilt? A fact that may shed light on this mystery is that, several times in the last decade, vandals have defaced her gravestone, which reads "Sylvia Plath Hughes," by erasing the word "Hughes."

In the court of public opinion, Ted Hughes is believed to bear responsibility for his wife's death. Yet an ever more punishing result than being called a "murderer," is that his identity is fixed as "Sylvia Plath's husband." Just as Sylvia is a martyr to the cause of Woman Scorned, so is Hughes a martyr to the cause of Suicide as Revenge. (He died of natural causes in 1998, within a year of the publication of his *mea culpa*.)

## LOST SOULS

The targets of suicide, such as the recalcitrant widows of Miller's study, the poignant widows of Wallace's study, Sue Chance, or Ted Hughes, were flawed judges of suicidal motivation. They misjudged their adversaries by underestimating the degree to which they were hated by them; or, they overlooked the adversary's devotion to the adage "Don't get mad, get even." Because of these and a hundred other miscalculations as the fateful day approached, they found themselves with no defense against the fury of the suicidal assault.

One is left with the certain knowledge that these penitents have paid a dreadful price.

What can we learn from this? Working with a threatener to thwart his or her suicidal plan before it develops into an impulsive act, we can take some lessons from the real-life cases presented here. The case of Chance's son, Jim, is especially instructive. Without presuming to judge Jim's grandfather, who very likely did the best he could to help, we can take the liberty of some second-guessing. When the threat of suicide was first heard, a year before Jim died, he should have:

1. taken the threat seriously;

2. paid attention to any signs that planning was underway; for example, did Jim speak of using a gun to kill himself, and how did he get access to a gun?;

3. explored, with Jim, the inventory of his significant relationships, present or past, to find the one most fraught with anger;

4. if the sick relationship was the one with Jim's mother (his daughter), he should have intervened to create some kind of truce between them;

5. if the mother would not cooperate, he should have concentrated on his own relationship with Jim, improving it to the point at which it would *take precedence* over the relationship with the mother;

6. showed Jim that his wish to punish his mother was futile because she was incapable of change, cruel because other people—including himself (the grandfather)—could be hurt, and would bring disgrace on Jim because his mother would

denounce him as a "traitor"—in fact, she might write a book exploiting his memory to prove herself blameless;

7. persuaded Jim to adopt a new way of living independently of the mother and beyond her influence, thus freeing him from her spell.

These prescriptives rely, of course, on the wisdom of hindsight. Presumably, none of these steps was taken, and as a result the curse of Dr. Chance was not broken. Jim gave his body back to his mother after 25 years. She will never evade the comment of her peers, "Her son killed himself you know."

You have seen how people who are only trying to be helpful may get caught in the "fallout" from a suicidal attack. The grandfather of Jim was maligned in print by his own daughter. Naturally, you don't want something like this to happen to you. As every caregiver suspects, the person for whom you are caring may turn against you for no apparent reason. Because the object of his or her hatred is indifferent or absent, a threatener may find a convenient substitute in you. "Displacement of anger onto a safe object" is a valid psychological phenomenon; a good example is when a boy who has been bullied by an older boy at school, goes home and bullies his younger brother. In your work with the threatener, it may be necessary to point out that your role is only to improve the relationship between the two adversaries. You don't want to be the target of a suicide yourself. You have no intention of joining the next of kin.

# XII. HOW I GOT TO HEAVEN

Morning has broken
Like the first morning,
Blackbird has spoken
Like the first bird.

Praise for the singing,
Praise for the morning,
Praise for them springing
Fresh from the world.

—Eleanor Farjeon and
Cat Stevens
"Morning Has Broken"

Abe Bernstein and his dog, Wesley, were out walking one day when they went straight up in the air. As they rose, some neighbors saw them: "They both were looking upward," said one, "as if they were trying to catch a glimpse of where they were going. It was a beautiful sight." The man and his dog were never seen again. People speculated about why a sensible man like Abe would do a thing like that, but no answers came. An eight-year-old girl probably gave the best explanation: "He went with his dog."

Rachel, Abe's wife, was overcome by grief. She had to be restrained throughout the Kaddish, even though her son, Trevor, who had rushed home from college, was there to console her. Abe's brother, Ira, made the eulogy. On the day after the service, two armed investigators from Animal Welfare arrived at the house to ask questions about a report of the "untimely demise of a canine entrusted to your care." Ira was quick to remind them that "There is no demise—just a disappearance," and Rachel showed them the door on grounds of *corpus delicti.*

Trevor went back to college and Rachel began her period of mourning, resigned to the prospect that it would never end. A few weeks later, Trevor telephoned to say that he wanted her to know about a strange thing that had been happening to him. After asking how she was feeling, because he was constantly worried about her since Dad "went," he began to describe a new and fascinating development. Trevor had bought a new screen-saver for his computer, an abstract design with moving circles that would seem to retreat away from the front of the screen in a labyrinthine pattern. Recently, he thought he saw, within the lines of the inwardly-spiraling circles, English words, written in capital letters and producing a series of sentences and paragraphs. This image would fade in and out, without warning and in no discernible arrangement. Trevor's mind boggled.

He decided to record these rapidly-changing messages on videotape, so that he could study them later, and each night he set his camera in front of the screen, wedging the "Record" button down so that it would continue while he slept. In the beginning, there was nothing on the tapes that resembled what he had first seen with his own eyes, and it was many days before he was able to refine his recording technique, so that a text could be made out when the tape speed was slowed.

Having explained this to his mother, Trevor read her the text of his first clear message:

> It was a long while before we could find our way through a certain . . . barrier. It's one that all travelers encounter, because it's when you realize *what you were leaving.* It takes time to assimilate hard facts like that, especially because it was only on the spur of the moment that we made plans to leave. My friend, who finally communicates with me in ways I can understand, tells me that what we were feeling

up here was grief, but I said 'No way, because I accept what
*is* instead of pining for what *was*. The ones who are grieving
are down there.' He didn't agree and started to whimper
softly, and I tried to console him. My friend can be senti-
mental at times.

"Then the image evaporated and the circles on the screen were
blank. What do you think, Mom?" "Oh, heavens, I don't know
what to think. Your father believed in many strange ways. That's
why I wasn't really surprised when he . . . when he went. I'm going
to call your Uncle Ira. Maybe he can figure out what this means."

More time passed, and Trevor's experiments with his computer screen were laid aside for pressing concerns like term papers
and exams. He next thought about the mysterious messages one
day when his mother called. She had apparently taken these "astral communications" more seriously than Trevor had. The moment he answered the phone, she began, breathlessly: "I had a talk
with your uncle. He said something awful about your father—
that he was acting like a 'weirdo' before he, you know, went . . . Ira
said that Dad was 'bonkers' ever since he joined the Masons, talking about passwords and secret handshakes and the Rosy Cross.
Nobody told me anything about *that*. Why, Trevor, why didn't I
know? Did you know? How could you treat a mother this way?"

"Just calm down," Trevor replied. "It's true that Dad and I
weren't close, but I want to be here for him if he tries to make
contact. That's why I tape the screen-saver every night."

"Nonsense," said Rachel. "Let me tell you something else,
young man. I never believed that story about him and Wesley just
rising up in the air. I think he's coming back. One of these days,
he'll jump out of wherever he's hiding and scare me half to death.
Your father is a *kook*."

"Now, Momma, Dad would never hurt you. He loved you."

"So? From that, what am I getting? You know very well that
the doctor gave Abe only six months to live, but to do this to me—
vanish. How should I feel?"

"I know, Momma. I'm sorry."

"Your father should be sorry. And let me tell you one more thing, Mr. Smarty Boy: those messages *did not* come from him. He hated computers. Forget about that screen. You should pay attention to your studies. I know what you're doing; you're staying up all night and playing Internet. Are you eating?"

Chastened, Trevor thanked his mother for calling. He had forgotten to tell her about something else that had been happening for a while. Some nights, his camera recorded short, disjointed phrases on the screen, none of which added up to a coherent message but, even so, were intriguing. He made a list of what he had seen so far:

CHECK THE OIL EVERY TIME.
SELL THE RENTAL.
WATCH IT, IRA.
MAKE TREVOR JOIN THE MASONS.
I DON'T HAVE TO WEAR SHOES.

Trevor suspected that these comments, in the form of asides, may have been sent from a different terminal than the main text.

Another period elapsed without any discernible signals from space. Then suddenly, without fanfare, came this greeting of hail and farewell:

> Dear Family:
> Warm greetings to you all. Thank you for your patience. I feel that I can finally tell you why I am here—here, and not with you, where my duty lies. I wanted to tell you from the moment when I first decided to . . . go. But, you will agree, I was not as articulate then as I am now. For this confession I have long had the desire, and at last I have the words.
>
> To put it simply, I knew it was time to leave. Each of us, eventually, must come to the rude awareness that time is running out. You cross a threshold, so to speak, when deny-

ing the inevitable feels like self-betrayal. From then on, you have a different point of view: your thoughts turn to finding a way to exit gracefully, and you begin to sketch out the plot of your own Act III.

What would you do if you saw the curtain begin to descend above you? One day, I went up to the roof of our building and looked down. 'That will do it,' I thought. 'Just a slight spring of the legs will get me over the side and then . . . ' The difficulty lay in the chance that someone would think it wasn't an accident. If it raised a suspicion of *intent* on my part, people might look for someone to blame: 'Of course, it was because of so-and-so.' If it looked as though I had killed myself, it would lead to a roundup of 'the usual suspects,' and someone would be made to suffer for neglecting me. Nothing could be more unfair. I wouldn't have it.

It occurred to me that I could just run away, disappear. But likely the skeptics would prefer to believe that I was *removed* by some malevolent force such as a tornado, or *abducted* by a mischievous band of gypsies. The outcome I wished to achieve was to be gone, to become absent. I wanted people to say 'He was here, but then he wasn't.' More than that, I wanted to be faithful, as long as I could, to my 'best friend.' I wanted people to say 'They were here, but then they went.'

After much meditation on the subject, I asked myself 'What if I refused to believe in gravity anymore?' The idea is that you can go anywhere, as long as you free yourself from what's holding you here. I concentrated as best I could, and soon found myself rising up, a few feet at first, and then to the tops of houses. My research was done secretly, in the middle of the night, until I had the speed and direction under control. I did it by force of will, and the eventual result was that I discovered where I am now, this spirit home—more a state of mind than a location.

If you're worrying about my best friend, whom I

dragged along on this adventure, I can tell you that our mutual respect is much improved in the short while since we took our leave. He has reassured me that he was ready to go. It may have been insensitive of me to take him with me, but I felt that we deserved our companionship, since we had become so loyal to each-other. The other day, he told me that coming here was a far, far better thing than he had ever done, and that he found a far, far better rest than he had ever known. I thought that sounded swell, until he told me he got it from a book. Such is life on the astral plane.

Before I close, my good buddy reminds me to ask your forgiveness for leaving you early, well in advance of your natural expectations, and for our melodramatic mode of departure. I, personally, feel I should emphasize that it was not because of anything you did. To sum up why I decided to go, it was because I wanted to die without killing myself, to leave without making a fuss.

May you live long and untroubled lives. Think of us often, and we'll be watching over you night and morning. We won't be getting in touch for a while; they're moving us to another part of the Realm which, I am sure, will be as pleasant as this lovely meadow where we are as I send these thoughts. The day is calm, with high-flying clouds . . .

Here, the transmission became too faint to read for a few seconds, and when it cleared Trevor could make out only three parting words and a signature:

Licks and barks,
Wesley

Moral: Heaven is the land where dogs can talk.

# XIII. EMERGENCIES

There's a somebody I'm longing to see.
I hope that he
Turns out to be
Someone who'll watch over me.

—George and Ira Gershwin,
"Someone to Watch Over Me"

As a fully-fledged Lifesaver, one who has a comprehensive view of what the task requires, and no illusions about the risk to yourself, you should be aware that there are times when special measures must be taken. In this kind of situation, you have no chance to "reason" with a person who is threatening suicide, and often no opportunity to improve the relationship between threatener and potential target. Two examples of special circumstances such as these are described in this chapter.

As an orienting concept, it will be useful to examine the sequence of thoughts, resolutions, and declarations that mark the decision-making process of a suicidal person, from the planning stage to the emergency moment. Figure 5. lists these steps in order:

**Figure 5.**

# MILESTONES

| | |
|---|---|
| *The Choice:* | "I'll do it my way." |
| *The Plan:* | "I'll wait until after her birthday." |
| *Testing:* | "I wonder who would care if I did it?" |
| *Philosophizing:* | "The way things are, it's the only thing to do." |
| *Laying a False Trail:* | "Don't worry about me. I'll be fine." |
| *Euphoria:* | "Isn't this a wonderful world?" |
| *Spacing Out:* | "Sometimes I look in the mirror and see myself as a child." |
| *Withdrawal:* | "I'd rather not talk about it." |
| *Doing It:* | "Come back this evening." |
| *Sticking to It:* | "Keep on, keep on, keep . . . " |

These milestones of suicidal thinking are useful to the process of prevention, because it is vitally important to know *how close* the person is to taking action. In the scenarios presented below, you will see that figuring out how much time is left can be critical.

## THE MAN ON THE LEDGE

Pete's best friend, Gary, is standing on a ledge outside of the tall building where he works. The police have questioned his co-workers and found out the names of several members of his immediate family; when they cannot reach any of them by telephone, they ask about other people who know him well, and Pete's name is given. Shocked, because he had no idea that Gary's troubles were so profound, Pete gets excused from work and rushes over to the building. When he arrives, the police are well-pleased to let him talk to Gary, because they have been trying with no success for hours. Pete asks them to move back from the windows and keep quiet, so that Gary will think they might have left, and he leans out a window cautiously and says softly, "Hey, buddy."

Gary is staring at the ground ten stories below, his eyes bulging and his face chalk white. Pete can see that he has made up his mind to jump, and is now trying to force himself to follow through. When Pete asks, as calmly as he can, "What happened?" and Gary says nothing, he says "When I saw you yesterday, you were cool." Pete rambles on along these lines, trying to get him to respond, at least to establish a connection. After a while, when it's clear that Gary is aware of who it is, and that his best friend is reaching out to him, Pete pushes: "Was it Valerie?"

Gary's grimace shows that it was, in fact, Valerie; and after a long pause he coughs and says, feebly "I don't want to talk about it." Note here that Pete has moved him a few steps back from the "Sticking to It" phase; this was due solely to his knowledge of Gary and his current situation, and as a result Pete has captured his attention. Emboldened to press his advantage, Pete asks "Did she move out again?" Vehemently, Gary says "I threw her out." "How come?," Pete asks, solicitously. "I caught her in bed with Jason" is the reply. "In your house?"

Without waiting for Gary's answer, Pete ducks back inside and tells a policeman to call Valerie Sloan and "get her down here at once." He gives them the number and looks out again. Gary has started to cry but, scarily, he has put one hand to his head and is perched more precariously than before. "Hang on," says Pete, "I don't want you to fall." With this, Gary looks startled and then seems to turn his thoughts inward. Even so, Pete notices, he puts his hand back against the wall to steady himself. Pete tries to buy some time by telling Gary an inane story about something that happened at his work today. His first intuition is that Valerie will have to apologize to Gary, but he isn't sure, knowing Valerie, that she will cooperate. Pete does know that there is no safety net below this ledge, and that if he goes out there himself, his friend might jump.

What seems like an hour passes, but it's only minutes before the police call Pete inside and tell him that Valerie has refused to come to rescue Gary, and in fact had slammed down the phone. Pete is on his own. He knows that the best chance he had of getting Gary to change his mind was to persuade Valerie to change her mind, say she was sorry, and ask Gary to forgive her. At the very least, she should have come here, and even if she said nothing she would have let Gary know that she cares about him. As it is, Pete will have to improvise, and so he lies: "I had the police call Jason—the son of a bitch–to get him to come out here so I could kick his butt; anyway, he chickened out." Gary thinks a bit and says, with a sigh, "It's not his fault, it's hers." Pete quickly replies: "The hell it is; that creep comes into your house and screws your girl and you don't want to put him away? . . . What *do* you want; for *me* to do it?"

Like a quarterback who looks across the field from receiver to receiver, following a planned progression, to find the open man and throw him a pass, Pete must change his tactics as circumstances change. He knows that he cannot get help from the reluctant Valerie, who is the object of Gary's anger and the primary target of his threat. The next best thing is to divert the anger away from Valerie to the villain Jason. After a pause to let Gary reflect on what he had said, Pete continues: "Here's my idea. We get that creep to come down to the bar tomorrow night and I'll get up on a table and tell everyone what a backstabber he is. Nobody will trust him after that." As he speaks, he reaches out his hand toward Gary, and as he waxes further on the same theme, extends his hand closer and closer to his friend.

By now, Pete has become a regular chatterbox, making sure that Gary keeps focused. The message is that Gary *must* do something about Jason. Pete well knows that, if Gary jumps, Valerie will be hurt more than anyone else, but Jason will have much to gain by it. Little by little, Gary is led to believe that Jason deserves to be punished, and it begins to make sense to him that the only way he can do that is by coming in from the ledge. Pressing his point, Pete says "I just remembered something: the other day, I saw Jason's wife on the street, and she said he went on a fishing trip and wouldn't be back for a week. Wait 'til she finds out about *this*."

When Gary touches Pete's outstretched hand and permits Pete to guide him in through the window, this ordeal will be over. From the standpoint of suicide prevention, some key elements can be identified. The most important thing is that, in the moment of crisis, Pete was "there" for Gary: he was on the scene, he showed up. His chief advantage was the relationship already established with Gary. This, by contrast with the presence of the police, increased by a hundredfold Gary's chances of staying alive (So often, when they try to help people, the police are unable to shake their image as adversaries.). Moreover, it was Pete's actions after he got there that proved decisive. Throughout, he concentrated on his friendship with Gary and his concern for Gary, using his knowledge of the current situation in his friend's life and calling on their shared associations to create an empathetic bond. What he did not do was crucial as well: he made no mention of jumping, suicide, or death, as if to convey that he didn't think of those things when thinking of Gary.

Even though Pete made some suggestions of tricks that he and Gary could play to "get even" with Jason, he was aware that they might never occur. While his long-term goal was to turn the heat of Gary's anger onto Jason, his short-term goal was simply to get him inside that window. Trashing Jason could wait; retribution could wait; death could wait.

# THE WOMAN IN THE BATHROOM

Sarah's aunt, who lives in a city about 50 miles away, calls her one day to ask for help. Sarah's cousin, Amy, is locked in the bathroom of their house, threatening suicide. Sarah and Amy have never had a close friendship, and in fact have not seen each-other for at least ten years. Sarah knows only that Amy has been going to college, off and on, for many years. She is astonished that her aunt would call her, but the aunt insists that, today when she asked Amy if there is anyone she admires, she said "my cousin Sarah."

It takes more than an hour for Sarah to drive to Amy's house, but by then Aunt Charlotte is frantic. She says that Amy has been locked in since the night before, and has responded to her questions only four or five times since. Each time Charlotte touches the door, Amy says "If you come in here, I'll kill you." About once an hour, Charlotte hears a nerve-shattering scream; the first time it happened, she demanded an explanation, and Amy said "I cut my wrist." (By all appearances, she has reached the "Doing It" phase.) Since then, there have been screams but no explanations.

In this situation, Sarah is trying to save the life of a person with whom she has no current relationship. Moreover, she has no advance knowledge of what relationships Amy does have, or what are the day-to-day circumstances of her life. They often played together on family visits when children, but that was before either woman had formed an adult persona. Right now, Sarah is only able to ask a few hurried questions of Amy's mother, whose repeated theme is that Amy feels that she is a failure whose life is worthless. A horrible scream interrupts this briefing, and Sarah rushes to the bathroom door.

"Amy, it's Sarah. Do you remember me?" No answer follows, and Sarah tries being jovial: "I'm your long-lost cousin." Another scream sends a chill through Sarah, who reacts by reflex with "What happened? Are you all right?" "Go away," says Amy. "No way," replies Sarah. "I'm not going anywhere. Aunt Charlotte told me that you admire me, and here I am." After a long pause with no screaming, she starts off in a new direction: "I feel that I hardly know you. But we sure did have a good time when we were kids. I guess we kept in touch now and then through my mom and your mom. But what *have* you been doing these days?" In short succession there follow three loud screams, each more piercing than the one before.

Sarah pauses again and decides to stop asking questions. She launches into a monologue about earlier meetings that she and Amy had, starting with the most recent event, which was the funeral of their grandmother. "I remember that you had a white linen dress with a lace collar, and I had never seen you looking so pretty; I told you so, remember? I cried so hard I got tears on your dress when you tried to console me. I was afraid I had ruined it. You were very brave, but I knew you were as broken up about losing Grammie as I was."

On and on goes Sarah, dredging up the most obscure memories of birthdays when one of them had visited the other, with incidents like the time when Sarah's mother left the cake in the oven too long and Dad had to use a fire extinguisher. As she warms to her task and her narrative of significant events in their early years unfolds, Sarah interjects a question now and then, desperately listening for some reply—anything—from Amy. She says, for example, "There was a kid who could never play with a toy without breaking it; they called him 'Binky'; what was his real name?" Sarah had an intuition that Amy might, at first, answer questions about trivia but not about anything remotely connected to "heavy stuff."

Using this method with sporadic success, Sarah is able to get Amy to say a word or two, and later respond to leading questions such as "Are you feeling lost?" with "yes" or "Did someone hurt you?" with "no." Haltingly, Amy reveals that, on her 30th birthday, she thought she was going to die; in fact, she fainted and had to be revived. She is convinced that she will never finish college, never have kids, and "never be a real person." When Sarah asks the operative question, "Whom do you hate?," Amy says "all of them."

From this answer, Sarah understands that each of Amy's friends and acquaintances, relatives and mentors, co-workers and neighbors has neglected her equally, and thus are equally potential targets.

When Amy finally unlocks the bathroom door, Sarah finds her fallen back against the tub, covered in blood and nearly unconscious. Amy has wrapped both arms in towels, and both are soaked in scarlet. With great relief, Sarah finds that she had cut across her wrists; if she had done as seriously suicidal people do, cutting the veins lengthwise, she would be dead by now from loss of blood. As it is, she will need a lot of stitches, a transfusion, and 72 hours of observation in the hospital, but she will survive. Sarah goes with her to the hospital, promising to return the next day.

Driving home, Sarah reflects on this powerful experience, a reverie not untouched by a certain resentment because of the fear that Amy had created, both in her mother and herself. Later that evening, she feels more tolerant of Amy's pathetic *crise du coeur*. It became clear that Amy's subconscious was correct in forcing her to realize that she had come to a crossroad in her life. By conventional standards, she *had* failed in most of life's tasks, and she *had* lost whatever support and sense of belonging she might once have had from people she knew. When Amy said that she hated "all of them," she revealed that every one of her relationships was malignant to some degree. By succeeding in renewing their dormant ties as cousins, Sarah gave her what amounted to a new relationship and, by extension, a new lease on life. If Amy needed to start over, she had already begun.

There are times when the rule "fix the broken relationship" cannot be followed to the letter. A broken relationship, such as that of Gary and Valerie, for example, can only be healed by an indirect route; or, it may prove ultimately incurable and should be discarded. By contrast, there may be no single most oppressive relationship, as with Amy, and the solution is for her to move her life in a new direction and find new relationships. Special circumstances such as these are likely to arise with no notice, and when they do will require the advanced skills of the Lifesaver First Class.

# XIV. DARLA'S SONG

What shall I do to win my lord again?
Good friend, go to him; for, by this
light of heaven,
I know not how I lost him . . .
Unkindness may do much;
And his unkindness may defeat my life,
But never taint my love.

—Shakespeare, "Othello"

There is no more touching lament than that of Desdemona, because it reminds every one of us of love unrequited. When our
love, freely given, is misunderstood or unappreciated, we are left
with the sad awareness of waste—of passion and time. In "Othello,"
his tragic story of love gone mad, Shakespeare gives us yet another
lesson in suicide. The ironic part is that, after having killed
Desdemona, Othello seeks sympathy for what he has done, asking
others to speak of him as " . . . one who loved not wisely but too
well." He kills himself in the end, but that doesn't deter us from
thinking that he loved neither wisely *nor* too well.

Shakespeare's fable sensitively and eloquently instructs us about
the twinned emotions of love and hate: Desdemona loving so much
that she died for her pains; Othello hating so much that he died
for his. Love and hate as polar opposites, force and counter-force,
alternate in every relationship. The prevailing energy field deter-
mines the balance between partners at any moment. What happens when the balance is upset was well described by William
Congreve, whose oft-misquoted couplet reads:

> Heaven has no Rage, like Love to
> Hatred turned,
> Nor Hell a Fury, like a Woman scorned.
> —*The Mourning Bride*, 1697

The story of Darla is a cautionary tale, showing how love can turn to hate, and how hatred can destroy everything.

Imagine a planet where, when a person commits suicide, an investigation is conducted to find out who was to blame. Because someone is always to blame, eventually someone will be arrested, accused, booked, incarcerated, tried and, if the evidence is sound, convicted. The charge is murder and the sentence is death. This is what happened to one unfortunate whose name was "Tor" (People's names in this story have been changed to protect the guilty.).

Darla, a 29-year-old woman, killed herself, and the logical suspect was her former lover, Tor. They had lived together for several years, and at one time were planning to marry. In recent months, they had become estranged, some said because Tor had found a new girlfriend. At the trial, Tor was questioned by the prosecutor:

PROSECUTOR: How did she die?

TOR: We were talking in her car. Suddenly, she started the motor, ran to the front, lifted the hood, put her hand in between the batteries, touched the metal with her other hand, and electrocuted herself.

PROSECUTOR: What did you do?

TOR: I was paralyzed with fear. For one thing, I was afraid to touch her or the car, because I could be killed, too. I got out carefully and looked for a police helicopter. There were a lot of them overhead, and as soon as I waved my arms, one came down. Thank God for the Sky Patrol.

PROSECUTOR: How did you feel?

TOR: Shattered.

As the trial unfolded, much testimony was presented from Darla's family and friends, saying how shocked and saddened they were by her loss, how they had loved her as a daughter, sister, best friend, neighbor, pupil, school chum, church member, loyal employee, etc. Their sorrow was genuinely heartfelt, as well as their conviction that she was not the kind of person who would do such a thing; they were bewildered to think that she had killed herself, and were certain that some evil force must have overtaken her.

These loved-ones and admirers of Darla were unanimous in their denunciations of Tor as a cruel and self-obsessed person, and they spared no adverbs in describing how insensitive he had been to her during their affair. They reported how abominably he had treated her in public, criticizing her unmercifully and calling her names. They described how, when he decided to end their affair, he had turned over all her belongings—including her weightlessness gear—to haulers from the public recycling plant. Some of her friends, on reflection, were not surprised that Darla had taken her own life, considering how coldly Tor had humiliated her and how systematically he had contrived to break her heart. When each of Tor's accusers was asked, by the prosecutor, why Darla had killed herself, each one blamed Tor's treatment of her, and when asked what made them so sure, each gave a version of this answer: "Well, she killed herself right in front of him." Besides, some people remarked that he hadn't shed a tear at her passing: as far as they could tell, he didn't care.

An equally-enthusiastic band of Tor's supporters were heard from. They described every one of his virtues in fulsome detail, and concluded that he had treated Darla as well as could be expected of any man who had decided to end an affair. His current girlfriend, Karla, sobbed on the stand as she professed her love for

Tor and recounted his anguish as he tried to figure out a consider-
ate way to manage the separation; in the end, he had chosen the
"quick and dirty" approach, believing that someday Darla would
appreciate his candor. And it was only when Darla couldn't accept
the inevitable that Tor was compelled to dispose of her things. He
had only agreed to go for a ride with Darla in her car to "say
goodbye properly" and perhaps even to "make peace."

The testimony on behalf of his good character by Tor's family
and friends, and especially his girlfriend, seemed to reassure the
jury that Tor was a well-meaning person who had become en-
meshed in a relationship that got out of hand. Their sympathies
were further aroused when a suicide note, in Darla's handwriting,
was read aloud in court by the attorney for Tor's defense. This
note, found on the desk in Darla's apartment and dated on the day
she died, said:

> May everyone forgive me for what I have chosen to do.
> Dearest Mother, you who grieve me the most, be assured
> that I will always love you—please see this choice as the only
> one left for me. Dad, you must be strong for Mom and
> protect her always. There is some money in the bank that
> you can use to take her to the islands for your anniversary.
> Dearest brother, please take my car and get it fixed, so that
> you can get out of the wreck you drive.
>
> I leave my jewelry to my niece, Oka, especially
> grandmother's pearls. For the rest of my junk, maybe some-
> one can use something.
>
> You may be curious about Tor and me, and let's just say
> it didn't "fly." As far as he is concerned, maybe someone can
> love him. I can't.
>
> Goodbye everyone. Take care. Be as good to each-other
> as I was to Tor—the rotten jerk.

Tor's attorney, when he had completed his reading of Darla's suicide note, moved immediately for a mistrial, arguing that since no

crime against Darla had occurred, Tor should be set free. But, wanting to study her note in more depth, the judge decided to adjourn the trial for the weekend. Given this respite, the prosecutor met with his colleagues for a strategy session. The result of their deliberations was to summon Inspector Bok, a member of a visiting police delegation from another galaxy, who was renowned for his skill as a detective. As soon as he was told the facts of the case, Bok announced: "We don't have it where I come from—suicide, I mean. It was outlawed some years ago, and the taboo is strictly enforced. When a person threatens suicide, he or she is taken aside and warned that, after death, complete and utter shame will be attached to his or her name. Every memory of the dead person will be tarnished by scorn and heaped with ridicule. The reason is that our society is repulsed by the very idea of suicide, because of its brutality to the living. Even so, you good people here have a suicide mystery, and I would be pleased to help you clear it up. The puzzle is dazzling to a detective's mind, because the identity of the false victim is known, but the true victim is unknown."

Getting down to the case at hand, Bok studied the available evidence and mused: "I recall a suicide that happened on our planet before the ban, when this dead person had tried very hard to conceal the identity of the person who was responsible for the death— that is, the true victim. Is it possible that our tragic heroine, Darla, left *two* notes?" The Prosecutor and his staff were astonished but attentive, asking Bok what would cause a person to do that. "To leave a public message *and* a private one," said the Inspector. "Why?" asked the Prosecutor. "Because the messages are very different."

Intrigued by the suggestion that there might be new words from the dead woman, the Prosecutor asked where such a note could be found if, indeed, there was one. Without hesitation, Bok replied: "You told me, I believe, that the woman and her lover, Tor, had lived together. But, in getting rid of her, the man had her clothes and other possessions cleared from his apartment. It's possible that some of *his* belongings remained in *her* apartment. Because she could not bear to part with them, and realized that her beloved would retrieve them someday, she may have used these clothes as a means of communication." "How?" "By hiding her message in an article of his clothing, where he would find it eventually and be forced to read it."

They searched the contents of Darla's closets, and found, in the inside breast pocket of one of Tor's suit jackets, an envelope with his name on it. When they read the note, they knew that they had what they needed to, in their way of putting it, "nail the bastard." The note said:

> Poor Tor:
>
> By the time you read this—if you ever do—I will have fried my brains for love of you. I read that a sudden jolt of electricity causes the breathing center to stop functioning, just long enough in most cases to make the person suffocate. Of course, if you got to me in time and gave me the Kiss of Life I would be alive now. I'm not, so you must not have tried.
>
> I'm so glad you didn't kiss me, because I know that your kiss belongs to Karla. That woman deserves you. One day you will kill her—just as you killed me. You will promise to love her and care for her the rest of her life, and when the next bitch catches your eye you will be gone again. But, before that, you will torture her as you did to me. SHE WILL FEEL THE FIRE.
>
> Why? Why did you have to put me down in front of people and say I'm stupid and frigid and ugly and too dumb to be a mother? Why did you shame me and make me feel that I had no right to be alive?
>
> You want to know the worst part? I know you're past caring, but know this: the worst part was how you looked at me—not only in front of them but when we were alone—that sneering look on your face as though you hated to look at me and wanted me dead. That was it, the way you looked

at me, that froze my blood and choked my spirit. When you last see me, I'll be gasping for breath but my soul will be dead—because you KILLED IT.

This I write to you because you are the only one who needs to know how I feel. No one must read it but you. It is my last will and testament—to you, who held my life in your hands.

While the prosecutor was reading those words in the courtroom, neither the loved-ones of Darla nor the supporters of Tor uttered a sound. Then there was a murmuring from both sections, rising to a roar from both, and finally the judge sent the lot of them into the corridor, fearing a riot. After deliberating for less than an hour, the jury delivered its verdict, "Guilty of Causing a Death," and Tor was led away. A few days later, the judge handed down his sentence: death by electrocution.

Some months went by, and near to the time when Tor was to be executed, the planetary ruler stepped into the case. Called The Orb, this ruler was known for the fairness of his decrees. He declared that Tor had committed a terrible crime: he had alienated the affections of an innocent girl, and cast her out in favor of another; worse than breaking her heart, he had stolen her spirit; he took away her life in cold blood. For him to die in exactly the way she died would be a fitting irony but, all things considered, putting him to death would be too good for him. By commuting Tor's execution in favor of life imprisonment, The Orb delivered his final judgment: "He hasn't suffered enough."

This story has no moral to enlighten the reader, beyond the facts of the incident itself. It is worth noting that it did not occur on another planet. It happened here.

# XV. THE DEATH OF SUICIDE

The last enemy
that shall be destroyed
is death.

–I Corinthians 15:26

In the closing pages of Hemingway's *For Whom the Bell Tolls*, Robert Jordan, an American fighting in the Spanish Civil War, lies on the ground in a forest, his leg shattered by his falling horse. He can't move. The enemy has his position surrounded and will be closing-in soon. He can kill himself with his gun or wait until they arrive and kill him. He chooses to force them to do it, because he feels that he has no right to take his own life. The story ends with Jordan waiting for his executioners, feeling "his heart beating against the pine needle floor of the forest." He is a man who knows all there is to know about suicide and decides against it. He greets death on his own terms.

Because each one of us can act upon our universally-shared suicidal thought at any time, and choose not to, we have at least some power over death. The freedom thus gained makes it possible to live our lives with gusto, because we don't have to look over our shoulders to see if death is hovering near. Should the Angel of Death appear, we can say, with confidence, "I thought of you before, but I decided I'm not ready." In this book we have seen how the possibility of killing ourselves opens a door through which we can find the reason for staying alive. At the end of this revelation, we shall find the meaning of life itself.

We started along this path for the solely practical purpose of

keeping someone whom we care about from doing something foolish. In the process, we have had to confront some disturbing facets
of human character. By way of summary, we acknowledged harsh
realities such as these:

- there are people who passionately hate other people;
- a person can use his or her death as a weapon;
- *voluntary* suicide is an act of spite.

The human character, in contrast with these deformities, has many
redeeming virtues, not the least of which is a capacity for change.
We have found that relationships can be changed, just as people
can be changed, and we are motivated to help by the certain knowledge that, unless there is change, someone will be hurt. Here, we
have explored some methods that can be used to make change
occur. In conclusion, the reader knows what to do when interven-
ing in a specific case of threatener and target. But what, in general
terms, can be done to deter people from making suicide threats in
the first place?

## THE GOAL

Someday, when the first Martian arrives, he might be found in the
New York Public Library, reading statistical reports of the World
Health Organization. Suddenly, he exclaims to the librarian: "What,
no suicide?" The librarian replies "Of course not, we're *evolved*."
Between now and the arrival of this visitor, what can we do to give
credence to the librarian's boast? What principles of creative evolution can we apply to the making of a civilization in which suicide
rarely happens? A good example of these principles at work in
improving the race is that of medical science in eradicating some
forms of disease. We can apply the same model to find a deterrent
to suicide. Any disease presents two challenges to the medical researcher: how to cure it and how to prevent it. In some cases, the
answer to one is the answer to the other, but in the absence of one

the other will do for a start. For instance, we could invest the greater part of our energy toward reversing the course of each case of AIDS, but eventually the goal is to find a way to make everyone impervious to the disease.

To some extent, Western culture is working toward giving people a kind of psychological immunity against the AIDS virus, by promoting "safe sex" on the part of every age group from puberty on up, and in nearly every social class; health advocates give out free condoms on the street, for example. Governments are acting to prevent the sharing of needles by drug users, in some places by providing sterile needles free. These approaches are absolutely necessary at the moment, because we are not likely to eradicate drug abuse soon and we have no intention of prohibiting sex. Meanwhile, biochemists are working fervently to find an actual cure or vaccine.

In America, we are even more serious about creating a stigma against smoking. This campaign began less than fifty years ago but has succeeded beyond a health planner's fondest expectation. A perfect example of the triumph of will over impulse, its guiding principle is the prospect of shame. It works by convincing people that, if they smoke in public, people will see them and ridicule them for doing it. Worse yet, if they do it in the vicinity of someone else, the second-hand smoke could actually harm the other person. The billboards that convey this message to the would-be smoker could not be more blunt. One shows a well-dressed man and woman conversing; he holds a cigarette in his hand and asks "Do you mind if I smoke?"; the woman replies: "Do you care if I die?" In another billboard picture, a smoking man says, to an elegant woman, "Your scent is intoxicating"; she replies "Yours is carcinogenic." Through advertisements such as these, expressing official government policy, the culture seeks to impose a powerful societal ban against an all-too-human form of self-indulgence.

# SHAME

Social deterrence based on the fear of being the object of ridicule or shame is vital to civilization, because it holds impulses in check while people ask themselves "What will they think of me?" This force is so powerful that, as with the taboo against incest, people in nearly every one of the world's cultures obey it without giving it more than a passing thought. In the Twenty-first Century, incest may become virtually unthinkable, in just the way that we no longer seek out witches and lust to burn them at the stake. This is how the human condition is improved by making certain urges taboo, and thoughts about them anathema.

This book proposes that preventing suicide relies heavily on the human emotion of shame. Shame is a powerful deterrent to the suicide motive because the suicidal person's bargain with death requires that people "get" what the act intended. Since the purpose of this death is to reveal and punish a villain among those who remain, the shame for this act is to be transferred to a survivor. But by reversing that process and causing the person to fear that shame will fall on him or her instead, a threatener may decide to cancel the bargain. The threatener must be guided to the reasoning that if he or she goes through with it, people will know why it happened, and no one will be confused about what the suicide meant to accomplish. Because these people will know why, they will refuse to let the act of suicide affect them in the way it was intended. Not only that, they will denounce it as evil and break their emotional ties with the deceased. Some will spit on the grave.

The promise of disgrace as a deterrent to suicide has certainly been given a chance in our culture. As recently as the 19th Century, a suicide would be buried at a crossroad with a stake through the body; the idea was that taking one's own life was a sign of weakness, allowing the Devil to take possession of the soul. In fact, suicide is an act of consummate rage, requiring a perverse inner strength, and dedication to the belief that better that getting mad is getting even. Now that we know why people do it, we may have the answer to getting it under control. One day it may be left behind, like cannibalism, as an ugly relic of the slow and fitful evolution of our race.

# THE ANSWER

When Watson and Crick, at Cambridge University, were studying the basic chemistry of hereditary transmission, their task was to find out how the pieces of Nature's puzzle combine to make up the DNA molecule. They knew that four chemical compounds— adenine, guanine, thymine, and cytosine—were present in some combination, but they had to figure out what that combination was. The solution to the puzzle, as we know, took the form of the double helix, a geometric model into which each component fit perfectly. In constructing the double helix, it was necessary to dis- cover which compound connects with each other one, and in what order. When their work was done, they had cracked the genetic code, a principle of Nature. as fundamental as gravity. In this book, three elements of human feeling—the emotion of shame, the will- ingness to apologize, and the impulse to forgive—are combined to form a deterrent to suicide. This vaccine will immunize people against killing themselves, because it is extracted from the root causes of suicide itself.

# THE DEATH OF LOVE

Suicide is inherently wrong when it does not consider the emo- tional damage that may be left in its wake. Note the limit case of what this act does to people: think of a child whose parent has committed suicide, a child who may not even understand the con- cept of death. Without warning or goodbye, a parent is gone from the child's life. He or she must process what has happened, place it in the context of whatever he or she knows about life, summarize his or her feelings toward the dead parent when alive, confront the loss, and create a new perspective on what life means and what the future holds in store. Regardless of how the child is able to "come through" this crisis of identity and resolve his or her conflict between grief and anger over abandonment, no child of suicide remains innocent of the horror of the world. It may be easy for most of us to banish the idea of suicide from our consciousness on most days, but the child of suicide lives with it, most days, like an affliction.

Among those who are most hurt by suicide, second only to the abandoned child, are people like the widows whose anguish was described above in Chapter XI. Because men outnumber women in killing themselves by a factor of four to one, the most likely bereft survivor is a woman who has lost a life partner to suicide. For most, this grief is beyond comprehension, the sense of desertion beyond despair. When a person makes a commitment to a partnership, to another life, he or she subscribes to the vow of "until death do us part" with no expectation that the death referred to could be *chosen*. Here is betrayal of the deepest trust. Whatever love there was between these people has consumed itself, like the fire from a bolt of lightning consumes the burning tree.

Finally, the third worst legacy of suicide falls upon the parent who has lost an adolescent or young person. This son or daughter who showed so much promise, who "had all of life ahead" is gone, and much of parenthood is gone as well. There may be other sons and daughters to fuss over or brood about, but the mother or father of a suicide will always doubt that he or she is suited to the parental role. We often see this epitomized in the families of celebrities, in which a son or daughter, despairing of ever achieving a fraction of the parent's fame, makes an early exit from the scene. The famous person then, in a press conference, blames drugs or mental illness. In the next act of this drama, the parent pledges support for a nationwide drive to stamp out mental illness or drug abuse, in a well-publicized bid for even more fame. The reason why a parent grieves so deeply for a child who has been lost to suicide is that parents, consciously or unconsciously, pride themselves on having "given" life. When that life is thrown away, the giver is defiled by the destruction of the gift. The result may be, as it was in the sad case of Dr. Chance, self-defense in perpetuity.

## GOODBYE TO ALL THAT

Suicide has been with us since the race began, and so have murder and thievery and betrayal and other crimes of the heart. We have come a long way toward civilizing ourselves, an endeavor that requires us to exert ever-tighter controls on human folly. No sooner do we attain a world without war or take a stand against terrorism or pass strict laws to prohibit child abuse, than we learn that we have merely eradicated one ill to expose another. And so it goes, as we discover over and over again what we knew from the start, that mankind is never perfect, only perfectible. When we think about this vast gulf between what we are and what we ought to be, it may be the closest we can come to a true contemplation of God. For God is everything that we cannot achieve.

William Booth, who founded the Salvation Army, was asked what, for him, was the most beautiful word in the English language. After a pause for reflection, he said "others." That word sounds the theme of this book, so often have I invoked it to signify the operative principle in suicide and the antidote to suicide. From medical science, we observe that a small element of a disease process can be used to immunize a person against the full-blown disease. In preventing suicide, the wish to hurt a loved-one can be transformed into the resolve to live *for* a loved-one. In short, others cause the impulse to die, and others are the motive for staying alive. If hate is stronger than love, someone may die, but love counters with the life-giving force.

Just as the one who loves and the loved-one are held together by an irresistible force, so are the hater and the object of hatred. This is the "mutuality" of the I-Thou bond that Martin Buber described so compellingly when he wrote: "Man becomes an I through a You." What it means is that personhood is reached through a series of encounters that we have with others. These define us and give each of us our unique identity. We exist "in relation to" and "because of." Who we are is how we interact one with another, and the story of a life is the chronicle of myriad encounters with others, in which our individuality is a collage of the perceptions of us in other minds. When a person *chooses* to die, he or she distorts and then obliterates the understanding and caring that at least one person had for him or her. To do that willfully is savage, evil, and just plain wrong.

When, in the Twenty-first Century we awaken one day to find that suicide is largely a thing of the past, the Lifesaver can be doubly proud. For if you save a life, you save a relationship. And the meaning of life is relationship.

# XVI. THE MEANING OF LIFE

No man is an island, entire of itself . . .
Any man's death diminishes me, because
I am involved in mankind;
And therefore never send to know for whom
the bell tolls; it tolls for thee.

—John Donne, "Devotions upon
Emergent Occasions"

*Alter est, ergo sum.* There is another, therefore I am. Self-aware-
ness begins with an awareness of others, and self-knowledge is
derived from comparing and contrasting inner feelings with
those perceived in others. We know who we really are by reflection from our experience of others. A child, for instance, lacks
this experience and thereby lacks this perspective. To begin
with, by differentiating yourself from others, you become who
you are. And then, with time and guidance, you discover who
that person is. They are the mirror. You are the image they give
back to you.

We begin and end a life with relationship, and each of our
joys along the way, not to mention our sorrows, is relation-
ship-bound and relationship-driven. Because other people define our existence, our existence is a quest to find out who we
are "in their eyes." Who are *you* in the eyes of your spouse or
loved-one, your child, your brother or sister, your father and
mother, your best friend? And, apart from this search for identity, what is the nature of your relationships with those persons? Are they loving or hateful, harsh or kind, giving or tak-

ing? And further, apart from how you are defined by them or treated by them, what do you give to them, these others? How have you enhanced the life of each one? In the words of Camus, my spirit-guide on this voyage, "We are meant to live for others." In that maxim, the word "for" carries the message. Whatever you give is a gift to yourself.

Far from being a naive altruism, this point of view casts light on the nature of existence. For example, when Paul Gauguin asked "Where do we come from? What are we? Where are we going?," his questions were attempts to clarify just what the Life Force "had in mind." Some would say that what the Life Force intended was that creatures on Earth would live, perpetuate their species, and thereby live on *ad infinitum*. I sense a different purpose, namely that the Life Force uses perpetuation of the species as a *means* to an end. The end is relationship. In short, life exists to make relationship possible.

Relationship, in its elemental form, requires no more than recognition of one creature by another. From it can develop, between members of a pair, patterns of interaction so complex in their configuration that, in the extreme of complexity, we need a Freud or Shakespeare to interpret them for us. At the opposite end of this continuum, we have the bond between mother and newborn child, which any observer can see with perfect clarity because it is expressed with looks and gesture and cannot be spoiled by words. Like it or not, relationship is; we are born into it or we acquire it, but it is as natural to life as breathing. The famous advice of E. M. Forster, "Only connect," is a truism, because there is no way not to connect. We are connected, we were connected, and we shall remain connected for the rest of our lives. In fact, having been connected may be the only legacy we shall ever leave after we are gone. In the words of the poet, Philip Larkin, "What will survive of us is love."[10]

Thinking about people in pairs, as connected entities, is not a

[10] Larkin, P. "An Arundel Tomb," In *Collected Poems*. New York: The Noonday Press, 1993, pp. 110,111.

routine perspective. It comes more naturally when a person dies, because then our first thought is about how his or her most significant other must feel—we focus on the connection. Suicide is another matter, because the connection is deliberately severed. When I looked carefully at the reality of suicide, it struck me that committing an act like that denies life's basic principle, just as not doing it affirms life. If people kill themselves to destroy a relationship, and stay alive to save a relationship, it follows that life and death are the ultimate polarities of relationship.

When you say to someone "I'll tell you about your life. Your life is the sum total of your relationships, then and now," the response may be "Is that all there is?" Indeed, isn't the purpose of life to acquire wealth or become famous or attain privilege or be honored by one's peers or "establish a dynasty" or prove one's virtue before God or Allah or Brahma or Buddha? Isn't life a race to be won or a trial to be endured? Isn't each of us an individual entity, governed in what we do by our personal commitment to our own god? Do we not, in the common wisdom, "come into this world alone, and leave alone"?

We can't and we don't—not since the beginning. God looked down at Adam, naked and afraid, and said "It is not good that the man should be alone; I will make him an help meet for him" (*Genesis*, 2:18). Along came Eve, and with her Adam's apotheosis. Since Eve, we inhabit a pluralistic existence of associations and dependencies, sharing and competing, in which we are continually obliged to ask "Who is that person and what does he mean to me?" Like it or not, *interdependence* is an inherent characteristic of the human condition. John Donne said it best in "No man is an island." Each one of us *belongs*.

Imagine that, today, a guardian angel gave you the gift to see what you will see on your dying day: you can know what your thoughts will be as the end comes. How will you judge yourself? What will be your last wish? If you could ask only one person to be with you in that moment, who would it be? If you could plan in advance your final words, what would you say? Questions such as these seldom trouble us in everyday life, because a powerful internal censor keeps us from dwelling on thoughts like these. In short, the taboo against facing up to death, its ugliness and treachery, is forceful and persistent. As a race, we are superstitious enough to fear that contemplating dying might be to "court" death, as if daring it to come.

And yet we inevitably *do* contemplate dying—what it feels like and what it means. We toy with it in our thoughts, like an ugly talisman that will not stay in its box. The *idea* forces itself upon consciousness, yielding sentiments from the ecclesiastical:

> Then shall the dust return to
> the earth as it was: and the spirit
> shall return unto God who gave it.

> —*Ecclesiastes*, 12;

to the self-promotional:

> Sunset and evening star,
> And one clear call for me!
> And may there be no moaning of the bar,
> When I put out to sea . . .

> —Alfred, Lord Tennyson
> "Crossing the Bar";

to the cynical:

> Dying
> Is an art, like everything else.
> I do it exceptionally well.

I do it so it feels like hell.
I do it so it feels real.
I guess you could say I've a call.

—Sylvia Plath
"Lady Lazarus";

to the inspirational:

Nothing in his life
Became him like the leaving it; he died
As one that had been studied in his death
To throw away the dearest thing he owed
As 'twere a careless trifle.

—Shakespeare, "Macbeth"

What these expressions of belief have in common is their self-referential nature, arising from the premise that one's death is an entirely personal possession––my dust, my spirit, my voyage, my art, my careless trifle. The source of this way of thinking is the egocentric faith that oneself is the center of the universe, and that whatever happens affects me or is insignificant. This is the mentality of the two-year-old child, and the principle on which is based the Catholic ritual of absolution, given voice in the Last Rites, also known as Extreme Unction.

In a conceivable scenario, a man lies dying by the side of a road, the victim of an automobile accident. He tells the paramedics that he is Catholic, and asks them to summon a priest. The priest arrives and bends down to the stricken man, saying (in Latin or English):

Through this holy anointing
May the Lord in His love and
mercy help you
With the grace of the Holy Spirit.

May the Lord who frees you from sin
Save you and raise you up.

—"Sacrament of the Anointing
of the Sick"

A fine sentiment indeed, but under the circumstances, how cold. While the man draws his last breaths, a stranger is prattling on about sin and grace and mercy. Noble concepts, yes, but far less than the stuff of a human bond. This is not merely a Catholic form of alienation, because most religions require a final reckoning with the deity before an impending death. It's a person's last chance, after all, to confess and be forgiven in this life as opposed to the next one.

But what of the others, the ones who are not there by the side of the road when the climactic moment comes? A priest represents God, not a family. Think of what the others are losing, as the man's life ebbs away. Who speaks for them? It occurs to me that the concept of sin refers to the act of leaving someone behind who needs you. If it happens by inadvertence, grace and mercy will follow. If done deliberately, shame on you; may the fires of hell await you. In a secular world, where the rules are Man's rules, this is the most we can say about sin and redemption.

Because we are not solitary creatures, when we are ready to leave someone else is involved. While death may not come in the presence of anyone else, we die *with* someone. In the case of the suicide, that other person is the enemy who must be punished; but, for most of us, the well-being of that other person is our major concern. Dying is part of the connection we have with this person, and by no means the end of the connection: so long as the other person lives, the connection lives. Death, therefore, is a message sent in the context of a relationship, to be interpreted by the other member of the relationship according to the secret terms of their bond.

Even if it does not belong to a god or, for that matter, the tax collector, my death does not belong to me. Just as a person's life involves the lives of others, dying is a social event. It follows that the last best act of dying is *saying goodbye*. And as with many tender moments in life, it is not so much what we say but how we say it. The words of this song may reflect what is to be done:

> Softly, I will leave you softly,
> For my heart would break
> If you should wake
> And see me go.
>
> So I leave you softly,
> Long before you miss me,
> Long before your arms can beg me stay
> For one more hour
> Or one more day.
>
> After all the years,
> I can't bear the tears
> To fall.
>
> So softly,
> As I leave you there,
> As I leave you there,
> As I leave you there.

> —H. Shaper and A. DeVita
> "Softly, As I Leave You"

The death of a loved-one is a possibility that each person has thought of in advance, perhaps in the very experience of falling in love in the first place. What we shall think about him or her, how we shall feel and what we shall say, is prepared in "the silence of the heart." Suppose a malevolent spirit took away, today, the person whom you love the most, forever. What will you think of the lost love, and what will become of you now that the loved-one is gone? When C. S. Lewis lost his wife of just a few years to cancer, he wrote these words:

> I look up in the night sky.
> Is anything more certain than that
> in all those vast times and spaces,
> if I were allowed to search them,
> I should nowhere find her face,
> her voice, her touch?

—C. S. Lewis
"A Grief Observed"

A face, a voice, a touch: these are the sun, moon, and stars of earthbound relationship. They are enough.

# INDEX

Moses, 38
*Mourning Bride, The* (Congreve), 136

Nature (personification), 37, 42, 67, 146
Nero, 54
New York Public Library, 143
*New Yorker,* 49n
*Numerous Ways of Saying 'No' to a Researcher of Suicide, The* (Miller), 111-2, 113n, 117

*Othello* (Shakespeare), 134

Plath, Sylvia. *See* Hughes, Sylvia Plath
Plato, 37
Preston, Douglas: *All the King's Sons,* 37
Puccini: *Turandot,* 11

Rage, 40, 49-51, 86, 98, 112, 136, 145.
     *See also* Anger; Hate
Relationships, 50-1, 55-6, 79, 80, 84-7, 96, 118, 126, 130, 133, 143, 149
*Religious Wars* (Erdrich), 61n
Rescuer. *See* Lifesaver
*Romeo and Juliet* (Shakespeare), 41-2
Rwandan refugees, 46-7, 52

*Sacrament of the Anointing of the Sick* (Catholic rite), 155
Salvation Army, The, 148
*San Francisco Chronicle,* **61**
*San Jose Mercury News,* 45
Scapegoat. *See* Target
Self-loathing, 49, 97
Seneca, 54
Shakespeare, William, 11, 151;
     *Macbeth,* 11, 154
     *A Midsummer Night's Dream,* 109

Printed in the United States
6225

9 780738 846101